AUSTRALIA REMEMBERS 2

Customs and Traditions of the Australian Defence Force

ALLISON PATERSON

BIG SKY PUBLISHING

www.bigskypublishing.com.au

Dedication

For all those who have served our wonderful country in conflict, peacekeeping, and in times of crisis.

To my father, Noel Marlow (1937-2020), thank you for passing on the values, customs and traditions which bind our family.

We acknowledge the traditional owners of country throughout Australia and recognise their continuing connection to land, waters and culture. We pay our respects to their Elders past, present and emerging.

First published 2021

Big Sky Publishing Pty Ltd
PO Box 303, Newport, NSW 2106, Australia
Phone: 1300 364 611
Email: info@bigskypublishing.com.au
Web: www.bigskypublishing.com.au

Cover Design and Typesetting: Think Productions

A catalogue record for this book is available from the National Library of Australia

National Library of Australia Cataloguing-in-Publication entry
Author: Allison Paterson
Title: Australia Remembers: Customs and Traditions of the Australian Defence Force
ISBN 978-1-922265-22-7(PB)
ISBN 978-1-922265-23-4(HB)

CONTENTS

Chapter 1

CUSTOMS AND TRADITIONS

People all over the world have different customs and traditions.

A custom is an activity that people from the same country, religion, **culture** or even smaller groups such as a school or family have performed for a long time, or it can be quite new. It is the way the people of the group usually act in certain circumstances.

It is difficult to tell the difference between a custom and a tradition. They are similar, and the words are often used in the same way. When a custom is handed down over generations it becomes a tradition. Traditions that are handed down also include beliefs, legends, stories and even songs.

We see a range of customs and traditions on special occasions and they exist in our daily lives, but we don't always notice them.

A Birthday Celebration (courtesy - Amy Paterson).

Why do we have customs and traditions?

Customs and traditions help to bind people together as a group. They provide links to the past that create a sense of belonging. They can make us feel proud, are ways of showing respect, or of celebrating and commemorating.

In Australia we have countless customs and traditions. Our population includes many different cultural groups including the Aboriginal and Torres Strait Islander people who have lived for thousands of years in Australia and its surrounding islands. When the ships of the First Fleet arrived in 1788, they brought people of the British culture. Since then, people from many different countries have chosen to settle in Australia or have arrived as refugees. All have brought new cultures and traditions with them.

DID YOU KNOW?

Over thousands of years, the various communities of Aboriginal and Torres Strait Islander peoples developed many traditions including a strong affinity to the land, water, sea, animals, plants, seasons and sky known as *country*. *Country* is a place of heritage, culture and belonging. To enter the *country* of another group required permission. Once granted, the visitors would be welcomed and allowed to travel safely. Today, a Welcome to Country ceremony is held at the beginning of formal events all over Australia. It is a sign of respect for the traditional owners of the land and is delivered by a local Elder or another representative of the community. The traditional owners are giving their blessing for the event. It can include a song, dance and a smoking ceremony.

An Acknowledgement of Country is also a sign of respect and can be given by non-Indigenous people.

Gubbi Gubbi Dancers at Booin Gari Festival, Noosaville 2016 (photography Uwe Wullfren).

Kabi Kabi custodian Lyndon Davis provides the Welcome to Country at the Booin Gari Festival, Noosaville, 2016 (photography Uwe Wullfren).

Does your school have customs and traditions? Can you list some?

Does your family have customs such as what you usually do in the school holidays, on the weekend or on Christmas Day?

Awakening of the Dragon

The Bendigo Easter Fair is one of Australia's oldest festivals, dating from 1871. It includes the Awakening of the Dragon, a tradition which celebrates Bendigo's long Chinese heritage. During the gold rushes of the 1850s, people from across the world raced to the goldfields, including many who came from China. Dragons are an important part of Chinese culture.

A smoking ceremony at HMAS Albatross (courtesy Navy News).

Awakening of the Dragon 'Sun Loong' - Bendigo Easter Parade 2019 (Liz Martin Photography).

The Australian Defence Force

Members of Australia's Federation Guard which is a ceremonial unit of the Australian Defence Force (courtesy Department of Defence).

The Australian Defence Force **(ADF)** is responsible for defending Australia, its people and our way of life.

The ADF was established in 1976 when the Australian Government placed the organisations of the Royal Australian Navy **(RAN)**, Australian Army and Royal Australian Air Force **(RAAF)** under a single headquarters. As well as defending Australia, the sailors, soldiers, and airmen and women of the ADF also help Australians and people from other countries in times of crisis, such as after a natural disaster.

The emblem of the Australian Defence Force. An anchor, swords and a wedge-tailed eagle represent the Navy, Army and Air Force. These symbols are above a boomerang and below a crest which features the seven-pointed Commonwealth, or Federation Star. Like the Australian National Flag, six points of the star represent each Australian state and the seventh represents the territories.

The Royal Australian Navy

After the First Fleet arrived in 1788, the British Royal Navy sent ships to protect the new colonies. In 1859, the Royal Navy established a dedicated **squadron** in Australian waters called the Australian Squadron, which was based in Sydney. Over time, the colonies of New South Wales, Victoria, Queensland and South Australia created their own naval forces. These navies combined after Federation and became known as the Commonwealth Naval Forces. The King of England granted Royal Assent in 1911, which allowed the Navy to use the 'Royal' title and the HMAS prefix (His/Her Majesty's Ship) on their vessels. The Royal Australian Navy (RAN) continued to be supported by the Royal Navy until the early years of World War II (1939–1945).

FAST FACT!

The Royal Australian Navy grew very quickly during World War II when Australia was threatened by Japanese forces. More ships were needed to protect Australia and its people. At its peak the RAN was the fourth largest navy in the world with just under 40,000 personnel and 337 vessels.

The Australian Army

The Australian Army has its origins in the first armed forces of colonial times. In 1901, the Australian colonies became a federated nation. Two years after Federation, the armies of the colonies were combined and named the Commonwealth Military Forces later renamed the Australian Military Forces. These forces were only allowed to serve on Australian soil. Two volunteer forces, both known as the **Australian Imperial Force (AIF)**, were created for service overseas during World War I and World War II. The Australian Regular Army was formed in 1947 and was supported by the Citizen Military Force, now known as the Army Reserve. The name Australian Army was introduced in 1980.

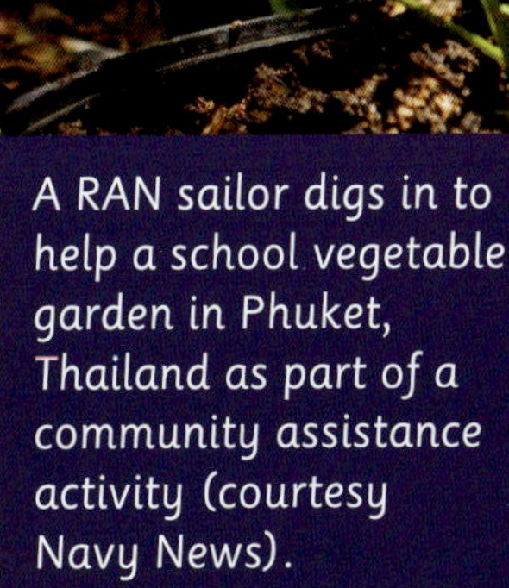

A RAN sailor digs in to help a school vegetable garden in Phuket, Thailand as part of a community assistance activity (courtesy Navy News).

Major Reynolds greets Lieutenant Harrison on return from a flight in the Central Flying School's Boxkite, Point Cook 1915. (courtesy RAAF Museum).

Royal Australian Air Force

The Royal Australian Air Force has its origins in the military flying school which was established at Point Cook in Victoria in 1914. In September 1912, the Australian Government decided to form the Australian Flying **Corps** which was attached to the AIF during World War I. The Australian Air Force was established in March 1921 and was independent of the Army. In August, the King granted by **royal decree** that it was to be called the Royal Australian Air Force. It is the second oldest independent air force in the world.

DID YOU KNOW?

The three Services have special words or phrases which have developed from customs, like the Navy using 'Aye Aye' to say yes! 'Aye' was old English for the word 'yes', while 'ahoy' was once the war cry of Vikings. Today 'ahoy there' is used to attract attention.

The customs and traditions of the Australian Defence Force are important to service personnel. There are hundreds of rituals, ways of behaving, beliefs and **symbols** that have been handed down, some can even be traced to Roman and Viking times, or earlier. Many of these practices were brought to Australia in 1788 when the first convict ships arrived from Britain. The Royal Navy and Marines brought customs and traditions which have become the foundation of many of the practices we see today, though some are unique to Australian service personnel, like wearing the Rising Sun Badge and the iconic slouch hat with an upturned brim.

> *If we don't have customs and traditions, we don't have a connection to the past; they are the basis of our discipline and what we believe.*
>
> David Gardner
> Director RAAF Museum Point Cook

Why are customs and traditions so important to the ADF?

As well as creating links to the past, customs and traditions provide service personnel with a sense of pride and identity. Members of the ADF are proud to serve Australia and its people. Customs and traditions also help to build respect and discipline.

Do you know anyone who has served in the Australian Defence Force?

Why do you think people want to enlist in the Australian Defence Force?

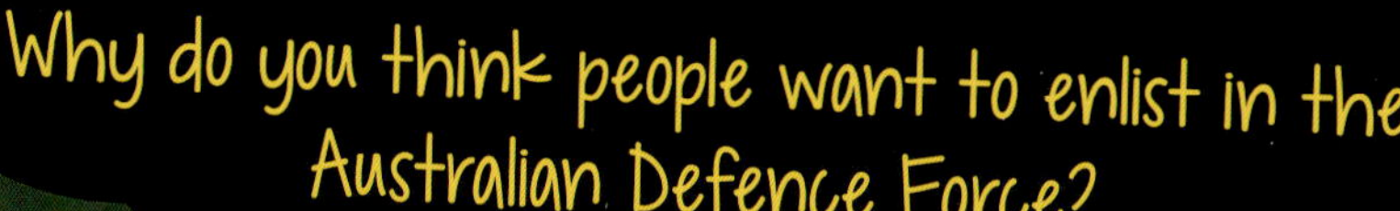

Graduation Parade of Staff at the Royal Military College, Duntroon – throwing hats in the air at a graduation ceremony is a tradition (courtesy Department of Defence).

A re-enactment of knights saluting each other.

Chapter 3

MISSIONS, MOTTOES AND CODES

Many organisations have a mission statement, a motto or code of behaviour that expresses a goal or a guiding principle. Mission statements and codes can be quite lengthy, while a motto is brief, sometimes just one word. There are many mottoes in the ADF, as each individual **unit** has its own. They can be written in different languages such as Latin, Welsh, French and German, as well as English and are inscribed on badges, embroidered on flags and within emblems. Most are based on traditions and values of the past.

The Australian Defence Force

The ADF has an official mission and role which the Australian Government created to guide their actions. There are lots of big words. It means that the ADF serves the people of Australia and keeps us safe.

Mission

The Australian Defence Force (ADF) is constituted under the Defence Act 1903, its mission is to defend Australia and its national interests. In fulfilling this mission, Defence serves the Government of the day and is accountable to the Commonwealth Parliament which represents the Australian people to efficiently and effectively carry out the Government's defence policy. (Commonwealth of Australia 2016).

The Values of the Australian Defence Force

Service. The selflessness of character to place the security and interests of our nation and its people ahead of my own.

Courage. The strength of character to say and do the right thing, always, especially in the face of adversity.

Respect. The humanity of character to value others and treat them with dignity.

Integrity. The consistency of character to align my thoughts, words and actions to do what is right.

Excellence. The willingness of character to strive each day to be the best I can be, both professionally and personally.

The badge of the Pilbara **Regiment** features the motto 'Mintu Wanta' which is an Aboriginal phrase that loosely means 'always alert' (courtesy Department of Defence).

The Motto of the Royal Australian Navy

Navy – *Serving Australia with pride*

A Seaman at Fleet Base West, Western Australia (courtesy Department of Defence).

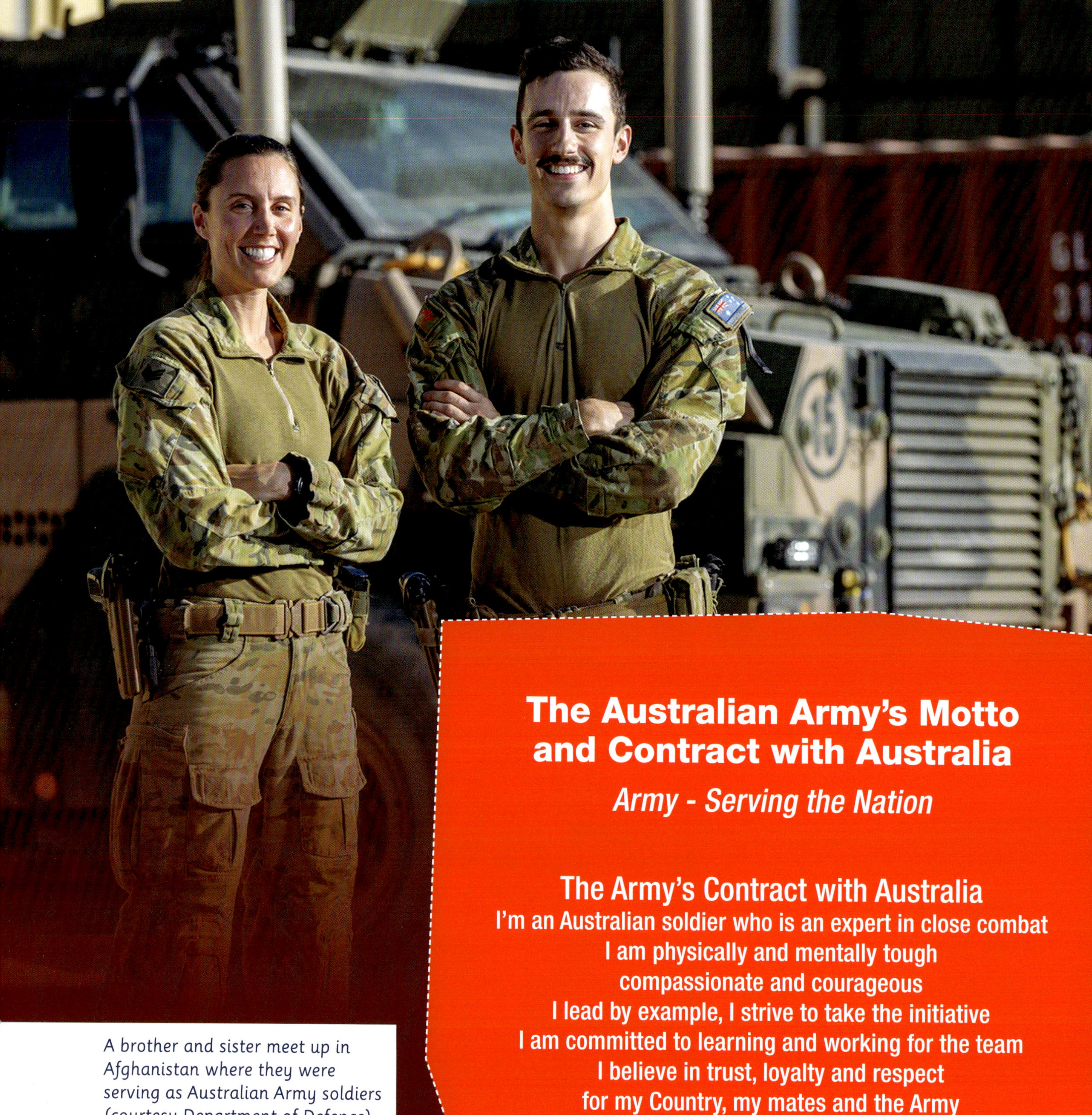

A brother and sister meet up in Afghanistan where they were serving as Australian Army soldiers (courtesy Department of Defence).

The Australian Army's Motto and Contract with Australia

Army - Serving the Nation

The Army's Contract with Australia

I'm an Australian soldier who is an expert in close combat
I am physically and mentally tough
compassionate and courageous
I lead by example, I strive to take the initiative
I am committed to learning and working for the team
I believe in trust, loyalty and respect
for my Country, my mates and the Army
the Rising Sun is my badge of honour
I am an Australian Soldier – always.

Does your school have an emblem or a motto?

Try writing a motto for yourself that can be a guide for your own choices and behaviour.

St Andrew's Anglican College Logo with Motto "with Vision and Spirit"

The Motto and Airman's Code of the Royal Australian Air Force

The RAAF motto *Per Ardua Ad Astra* is Latin and originated from the British Royal Air Force motto. It means 'Through adversity to the stars'.

The Airman's Code

I am an Australian Airman
I inherit a proud tradition
I follow in the footsteps of many fine Australians
Their legacy is my future

I am an Australian Airman
The air is our domain
I strive for excellence in all that I do
To protect our skies, our country, the land I love

I am an Australian Airman
I live for my family, work with my mates,
Support my community and fight for my nation
I am a valued member of the Air Force team
I do what is right

I am an Australian Airman

Members of RAAF serving in the Middle East (courtesy Department of Defence).

Chapter 4

Commemorative Services

Commemorative services like those held on Anzac Day and Remembrance Day follow a structure which is highly valued and practised in many countries. The rituals performed at commemorative services are based on traditions passed down through generations, even centuries, and have fascinating origins and meanings.

The Structure of a Commemorative Service

1. Introduction
2. Catafalque party is mounted
3. Commemorative Address
4. Hymn, prayer, reading and/or poem
5. Wreath or poppy laying
6. The Ode of Remembrance
7. Last Post
8. Period of silence followed by the raising of the flag
9. Rouse
10. National Anthem
11. Catafalque Party dismounts

An Australian Army Slouch hat sits on a commemorative stone (courtesy Department of Defence).

Why do members of the ADF stand at the corners of a war memorial at Anzac Day and Remembrance Day services?

This is called the mounting of the catafalque (pronounced 'cat-a-falk') party. A catafalque is a raised support for a coffin. A catafalque party was originally intended to guard the coffin of an important person. In commemorative services today, four members of the ADF slowly march in and position themselves on the corners of the remembrance stone, **cenotaph** or **memorial**. The cenotaph or memorial is the symbolic grave of all those who have lost their lives, while a remembrance stone represents the catafalque and coffin. The catafalque party is a symbol to show we protect the memory of those who gave their lives.

Why do they stand so still with their guns pointing down?

Reversing and resting on arms is a sign of respect or **mourning** and is thought to have originated in ancient Greece. The first recorded example of reversing a weapon and leaning on it at a military funeral was in the 16th century.

The catafalque party at the Australian National Memorial, Villers-Bretonneux, Anzac Day 2019 (courtesy Navy News).

The catalfaque party rests on arms during an Anzac Day Dawn Service in Iraq 2008 (courtesy Department of Defence).

Why is the poem 'In Flanders' Fields' read on Anzac Day and Remembrance Day?

The poem 'In Flanders' Fields' was written in 1915 by Lieutenant Colonel John McCrae, a medical officer in the First Canadian Army. It became one of the best known war poems of all time. It reminds us of the enormous sacrifices that are made, of the responsibility to always be grateful, and remember those who have served our country.

In Flanders' fields the poppies blow
Between the crosses, row on row,
That mark our place; and in the sky
The larks, still bravely singing, fly
Scarce heard amid the guns below.
We are the dead. Short days ago
We lived, felt dawn, saw sunset glow,
Loved, and were loved, and now we lie
In Flanders' fields.

Take up our quarrel with the foe:
To you from failing hands we throw
The torch; be yours to hold it high.
If ye break faith with us who die,
We shall not sleep, though poppies grow
In Flanders' fields.

A catafalque party member rests on arms at the Anzac Day Dawn Service on board HMAS *Canberra*, Malaysia (courtesy Navy News).

A member of a catafalque party performs Reversed Arms (courtesy Department of Defence).

Why do we wear poppies on Remembrance Day?

The poppy commemorates those who have given their lives in war and is the international memorial flower worn on Remembrance Day. Wearing a single poppy is a sign that we remember the sacrifices made by others for our freedom and safety. We also lay wreaths during memorial services, including Anzac Day, which are made of poppies or other flowers.

Wild poppies grew on the battlefields of Gallipoli, France and Belgium. In 1918, an American woman, Moina Michael, read the poem **'In Flanders Fields'**, then wrote a poem called **'We Shall Keep the Faith'**. She described red poppies as being a symbol of the blood of the soldiers. She chose to always wear a red poppy. A French woman named Madame Guérin later suggested the creation and sale of artificial poppies as a fundraiser for ex-**servicemen**, women and their children. A tradition had begun!

Wreaths, Villers-Bretonneux National Memorial, France, Anzac Day 2011.

The Ode of Remembrance

The Ode is the fourth stanza of the poem, ‘For the Fallen’, written in September 1914 by Laurence Binyon. It is our pledge to remember and honour those who have given their lives while serving our country.

They shall not grow old, as we that are left grow old;
Age shall not weary them, nor the years condemn.
At the going down of the sun and in the morning
We will remember them.

The people attending the service then repeat:

We will remember them.

Sailors stand in silence around the Pool of Reflection during a Last Post Ceremony at the Australian War Memorial 2019 (courtesy Department of Defence).

The Bugle Calls

There are many kinds of bugle calls. The three that can be heard on Remembrance Day and Anzac Day are:

The **Last Post** signals the end of the day. In the commemorative service it is a final farewell, a symbol that the duty of the dead is over, and they can rest peacefully.

The **Rouse** is played during a daytime service. It signifies that, after a period of mourning, our life and duty will continue.

The **Reveille** marks the beginning of the day and is sounded at a dawn service in place of the Rouse.

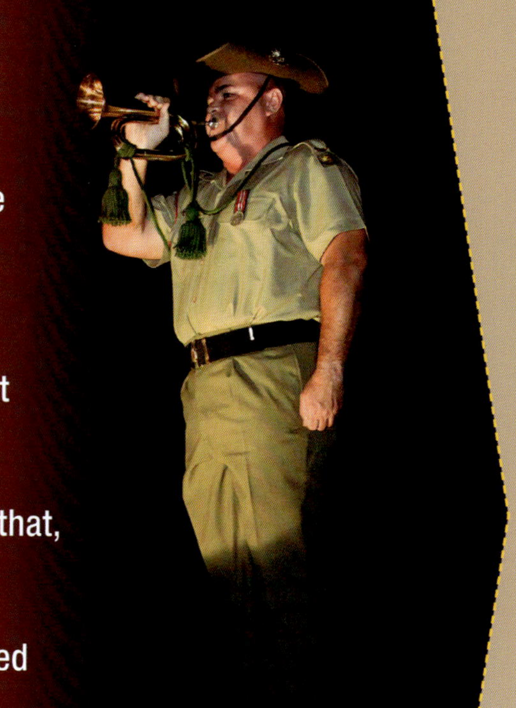

The Playing of the Last Post

One Minute's Silence

The tradition of standing in silence after the Last Post began on 11 November 1919. An Australian journalist, Edward Honey, suggested that we should have five minutes of silence on **Armistice** Day (changed to be called Remembrance Day in WWII). Sir Percy Fitzpatrick, from South Africa, also recommended a period of silence to recognise those who gave their lives. King George V agreed, declaring that everyone should stop in a 'complete suspension of all our normal activities' for two minutes at 'the eleventh hour of the eleventh day of the eleventh month'. In 1997, the Governor-General of Australia, Sir William Deane, officially recognised 11 November as Remembrance Day. He recommended that Australians should observe one minute of silence at 11.00 am.

In the Australian War Memorial, the silence gave me time to reflect on my great-grandparents who fought in World War II. It made me proud and sad to think about how the war changed not only their lives but others in their generation. And then I felt grateful for living in a peaceful time and I wish that it was the same for them.

Lucy Bowen

DID YOU KNOW?

The tradition of holding a service in the Commemorative Courtyard of the Australian War Memorial occurs every night. The courtyard also has a pool of reflection with an eternal flame. The flame is a symbol of eternal life and of Australia's endless gratitude and commitment to always remember those who gave their lives.

The Hall of Memory contains many symbols, including the Tomb of the Unknown Australian Soldier. Between 9 and 13 million soldiers from all over the world were killed during World War I. It is thought that one third of these soldiers have no known grave. Tombs of unknown soldiers are at other memorials throughout the world including Westminster Abbey in London and the Arc de Triomphe in France.

A soldier rests on arms at the Tomb of the Unknown Soldier, the Australian War Memorial, 2019 (courtesy Department of Defence).

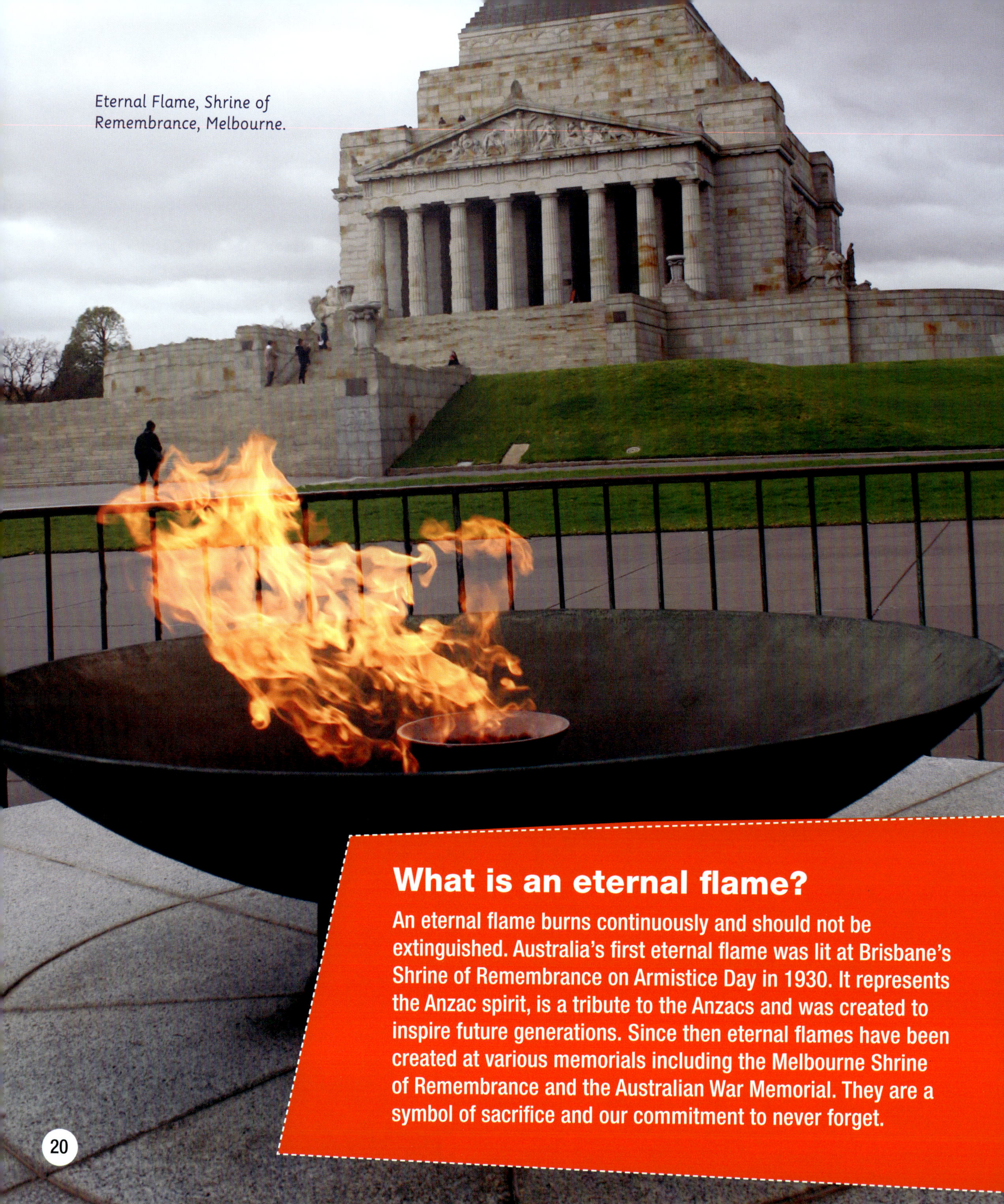

Eternal Flame, Shrine of Remembrance, Melbourne.

What is an eternal flame?

An eternal flame burns continuously and should not be extinguished. Australia's first eternal flame was lit at Brisbane's Shrine of Remembrance on Armistice Day in 1930. It represents the Anzac spirit, is a tribute to the Anzacs and was created to inspire future generations. Since then eternal flames have been created at various memorials including the Melbourne Shrine of Remembrance and the Australian War Memorial. They are a symbol of sacrifice and our commitment to never forget.

Lest We Forget wreath.

Lest We Forget

The words 'lest we forget' appear on war memorials and are recited during commemorative services and ceremonies. It is a pledge or promise never to forget the sacrifices others have made for the life we have today. It is thought that the words can be linked to Rudyard Kipling's 1897 poem 'Recessional'. The poem repeats the phrase 'lest we forget'. Kipling may have been inspired by a bible passage which used the words '… lest thou forget the LORD'.

Shrine of Remembrance, Anzac Square, Brisbane. The eternal flame is burning in the middle of the Shrine. (courtesy Rebecca Gray)

Anzac Day

The commemoration of Anzac Day is a tradition unique to Australia and New Zealand which began over a century ago in 1916. It marks the day of 25 April, 1915 when Australian and New Zealand forces began their first military action of World War I. On this day, in the early hours of the morning, the submarine of the Royal Australian Navy, the HMAS *AE2*, broke through the Turkish defences of the narrow Dardanelles Strait on the Gallipoli Peninsula. The landing at Gallipoli of the Australian Imperial Force, New Zealand and other allied forces followed. The **campaign** was ill-fated, the HMAS *AE2* and its crew were lost and months of fierce fighting resulted in heavy casualties before the Allied forces withdrew.

Anzac Day began as a commemorative service. Citizens and soldiers wanted to remember and honour those who had served or lost their lives at Gallipoli. By 1927 it had become a public holiday and by the mid-1930s the traditions we know today had become part of Australian culture.

Today, on Anzac Day, we remember all members of the ADF who have served Australia in wars, **conflicts**, or on **peacekeeping** missions.

My feelings marching on Anzac Day.

I march with spirit free, strong and Aussie pride with my medals on my chest. I march with my mates bonded in war and we march with our heads held high. We talk of our mates, deeds, laughs and often shed a tear. I remember my mates no longer marching, their memory stronger, my head bowed and silently remember the heroes' debt we owe, not a love of war but freedom, peace, prosperity.

Corporal Dave Morgan,
Australian Army, Vietnam

Why is the word Anzac sometimes written in capitals like this – ANZAC?

ANZAC is an acronym that stands for Australian and New Zealand Army Corps which was first used in 1915. Over time, the acronym became the word Anzac. The word is also used to describe a set of positive values, or spirit which the first Anzacs displayed. Australian sailors and airmen also served during World War I and even though the acronym ANZAC uses the word 'army', Anzac Day is an Australian tradition that includes all members of the ADF. The word Anzac is so significant to Australians that special laws exist to protect how the word is used.

The Anzac Spirit

The Anzac spirit is a tradition which refers to a set of character strengths. It is a **legacy** which has become an important part of our national identity. The original Anzacs displayed courage, mateship, resourcefulness, endurance and sacrifice. Many people believe these qualities have helped to form our traditions, our culture and our thoughts on what it means to be an Australian.

What does the Anzac spirit mean to you and your family?

Do you see people displaying the qualities of the Anzac spirit today?

Compare the qualities of the Anzac spirit to the values, mottoes and codes of behaviour of the Navy, Army and Air Force. What do you notice?

Do you think the Anzac spirit has played a role in developing our Australian culture?

> *Anzac stood, and still stands, for reckless valour in a good cause, for enterprise, resourcefulness, fidelity, comradeship and endurance that will never own defeat.*
>
> C.E.W. Bean (1946)

An Anzac Day Service at Lone Pine, Gallipoli 2019 (courtesy Department of Defence).

DID YOU KNOW?

A legacy can be anything handed down from one person or group to another. It could be personal property or something that affects or has a consequence for today.

Are you involved in any sporting clubs or other groups that have their own customs and traditions?

Veteran wearing rosemary Anzac Day, Tewantin 2019.

Rosemary.

Why do some people pin rosemary to their clothes on Anzac Day?

Rosemary grew wild on the battlefields at Gallipoli and is a herb that signifies remembrance. We wear it as a sign that we will never forget. People also wear rosemary on Remembrance Day.

Anzac biscuits.

Why do we make Anzac biscuits on Anzac Day?

Making Anzac biscuits is a tradition that began in World War I. During the war, family and friends at home would send parcels of supplies such as soap, socks, writing paper, fruit cakes and biscuits to those serving overseas. Anzac biscuits are made of oats, flour, sugar, golden syrup and coconut and stayed fresh for a long time. Recipes have sometimes been passed down from one generation to another.

Two-up on Anzac Day

Two-up is a game of chance that was very popular amongst the Anzacs. Two, or three coins, usually pennies, which are no longer part of Australia's currency, are tossed in the air from a piece of wood called the 'kip'. The person who tosses the coins is called the 'spinner'. Players try to guess whether two heads or two tails will land facing up, or on non-matching sides. Today it has become a tradition to play Two-up after Anzac Day services in places like RSL Clubs.

Australian soldiers play a game of Two-up in WWI.

Do you think Anzac Day will always be an Australian tradition?

Anzac Day has become a tradition in Australia and is a public holiday. What do you do on Anzac Day to commemorate those who have served Australia?

Lone Pine Memorial, Gallipoli

Why does my school have a pine tree called the Lone Pine?

In August 1915, the Anzacs suffered heavy losses in the Battle of Lone Pine at Gallipoli. Lone Pine was named after the single Aleppo pine tree that remained on a hill after most of the trees had been cut down to build trenches. Some Anzacs collected pine cones from the battlefield. Lance Corporal Benjamin Smith sent a pine cone home to his mother after his brother was killed in the battle. Smith's mother grew two seedlings, one was planted at the Australian War Memorial to honour all the sons who died at Lone Pine. Another soldier, Sergeant Keith McDowell, collected a pine cone and kept it for the rest of the war. A seedling grown from his pine cone was planted at Melbourne's Shrine of Remembrance. Trees from these pine cones continue to be planted in schools, at memorials and in the grounds of other organisations across Australia.

Why did the name Armistice Day change to Remembrance Day?

The name of Armistice Day was changed to Remembrance Day to include those who were suffering or serving during World War II. Today we remember people all over the world who have served and suffered in wars.

An Anzac Day Dawn Service, Greenwell Point NSW 2019 (courtesy Department of Defence).

Remembrance Day

The tradition of Remembrance Day began in 1919, when it was originally called Armistice Day. The eleventh hour of the eleventh day of the eleventh month marks the time in 1918 when a ceasefire was declared and World War I ended. The **Armistice** was signed at 5.00 am with all fighting to stop at 11.00 am. Remembrance Day is marked by commemorative services and ceremonies in Australia and in many countries throughout the world.

Why do we have a dawn service on Anzac Day but not on Remembrance Day?

The Anzac Day Dawn Service is a tradition in Australia and New Zealand. It marks the time and date when the first Anzacs landed at Gallipoli. Remembrance Day marks the end of World War I and is commemorated by many countries across the world. The first official dawn service is believed to have been held at the Sydney Cenotaph. Early in the morning of Anzac Day in 1927, a group of returned soldiers saw a lady placing a wreath at the construction site of the Sydney Cenotaph. The veterans decided to arrange a dawn service there the following year. Other forms of early morning services also happened across the country, even before 1927. By the early 1930s, dawn services were being held in the capital cities and many towns across Australia. A tradition had begun.

Reversing Boots in Saddle Stirrups (AWM 087280).

DID YOU KNOW?

The lone charger, a riderless horse, often leads parades at Anzac Day and other commemorative services, including funerals of important commanders. A pair of boots is placed backwards in the stirrups to represent the commander looking back on his troops for the last time. In Australia, the lone charger is a symbol of respect and mourning, particularly for the men of the Light Horse units. The tradition can be traced to ancient times. A great warrior's horse might be buried with him so that the horse would continue to serve its master. In some places in the world this continued until the 18th century!

DID YOU KNOW?

People who have served in the armed forces are called veterans. At commemorative services, veterans place their hand over their heart as a sign of respect or remembrance for fallen comrades. This tradition is called the Hand on Heart Salute. It is thought that it began in London on Armistice Day in 1920, at the opening of the Whitehall Cenotaph. All veterans, including recipients of the Victoria Cross, the highest award for valour in war, were requested to salute by placing their hand over their medals. This showed that the highest honour received could not be compared to giving one's life to serve others.

Apart from Anzac Day and Remembrance Day services, are there events you attend at school, or with your family, that also involve customs and traditions?

Students attend a Remembrance Day service in Brisbane 2018 (courtesy Department of Defence).

Chapter 5

MILITARY MUSIC AND INSTRUMENTS

Musical instruments such as drums, horns, whistles, bells and bugles have been used to communicate with soldiers and sailors since ancient times and are an important part of military life. Military musicians also provide music to march to and to simply entertain. Today we have modern technology to convey messages which means military music is mostly ceremonial, and for entertainment!

Drums

Drums have been used to arouse fear in the enemy and convey messages in battle since ancient times. Communicating with other groups over long distances was possible using the drum. Drums were also used to keep a steady beat when marching and to signal daily events in the life of a soldier. Today, drums are a significant part of ceremonies and parades.

The Combined Military Bands of the Australian Defence Force (courtesy Department of Defence).

All three Services of the ADF have military bands which perform on ceremonial occasions, at concerts and community events. Bands help create a sense of pride and build morale. Band performances also promote the work of the ADF within the community.

Did You Know?

A marching band is led by a Drum Major who is the person responsible for the band. This role has existed since the 17th century. Today, the Drum Major carries a mace rather than a cane or stick as they once did. The Drum Major does not play the drums, but often has two drumsticks secured to a sash draped across his/her uniform.

A Drum Major leads the Band of the Royal Military College, Canberra, 2016 (courtesy Department of Defence).

FAST FACT!

The Navy also used signalling flags and flashing lights (Aldis Lantern) to pass orders from ship to ship or ship to shore.

Military Bugle (courtesy Department of Defence).

Horns, Bugles and Pipes

Horns were also used to convey messages and signal events in the same way as drums. Horns were eventually replaced by bugles. In the Navy, the orders and messages were often conveyed by the Boatswain's (Bosun's) Call, a type of whistle. There are many different bugle calls including Fall in, Mess Calls (at mealtimes), Get Up! (Wakey Wakey!) and Lights Out. Those we hear at commemorative services are the Last Post, Rouse and Reveille.

The bugle that was used during the landing at Gallipoli (courtesy Department of Defence).

DID YOU KNOW?

Units can have their own marching music. The songs they march to vary from traditional ones of times past to more modern songs. The Royal Australian Army Dental Corps has developed the custom of marching to 'Puff the Magic Dragon'!

Why are the bagpipes often played on Anzac Day and Remembrance Day?

Scottish bagpipes are commonly used at ceremonies and parades. Many Scottish people came to Australia in the early years of settlement. The armies of the separate colonies had Scottish **Regiments** which we still have today. The tradition of wearing kilts and playing bagpipes remains.

FAST FACT

In 1746, when England was at war with the people of the Scottish Highlands, the bagpipes were declared a weapon of war by the English and were banned from use in Scotland!

How does the sound of bagpipes playing make you feel?

What song would you choose to march to?

Scottish Pipe Band - Anzac Day, Tewantin 2019.

Boatswain's Call

In the days of sailing ships, the boatswain oversaw the sails and rigging and issued commands to sailors using a Boatswain's Call. Shaped like a pipe, and sometimes called that, the Boatswain's Call emits a high-pitched whistle and can be heard above the sound of the sea. Changes in pitch are signals for different commands and are made by opening and closing the hand over a hole in the round ball (the buoy) at the end of the pipe. Today, the boatswain's call plays an important role in naval customs and traditions.

The Boatswain's call (courtesy Department of Defence).

The Ship's Bell

The ship's bell is inscribed with the name of the ship and the year it was launched. Bells have been used to indicate the time, for communicating with the crew, and as a signal for ships in fog or at night. The naval day is divided into 'watches' which are marked by the tolling of the bell for keeping watch and navigation. Ships' bells were usually placed at the base of the main mast on sailing ships. Sometimes an altar might be found there too, and so the idea developed that the ship's 'soul' was located at the base of the mast. Upturned ships' bells are even used to baptise the babies of sailors!

How does your school signal the daily routine?

Does your school have a band? Is its purpose similar to that of a military band today?

Did You Know?

Whistling is not allowed on board a naval ship. This is in case the sound is confused with a command from the Boatswain's Call.

PROTECTOR 1884

A Ship's Bell, HMCS *Protector* was a light cruiser commissioned by the South Australian Naval Forces in 1884.

Chapter 6

CEREMONIAL PARADES, DRILLS & SALUTES

Military Parades

A military parade is a formation of defence personnel to celebrate or commemorate a specific event such as Anzac Day or Remembrance Day. Parades are also held for events such as troops returning from overseas service, the arrival of a warship in its home port, a graduation ceremony, or simply for entertainment. Traditional marches and manoeuvres called drills are performed, as well as salutes which can include musical salutes, sword or rifle salutes and hand salutes.

The Queen's Silver Jubilee Parade, Canberra 1977 (courtesy - Retired Admiral Max Hancock).

Turn Out the Guard Ceremony

The Turn Out the Guard Ceremony can be traced to medieval times when guards were positioned to protect the gates of a city. When armed parties approached, the guards would 'turn out'. They also stood to arms ready for battle at dawn and dusk, the times when an attack was most likely — this is known as 'Stand-to' and 'Stand-to-Arms'. Today this tradition is used to greet or farewell important people and might involve an inspection of the guard.

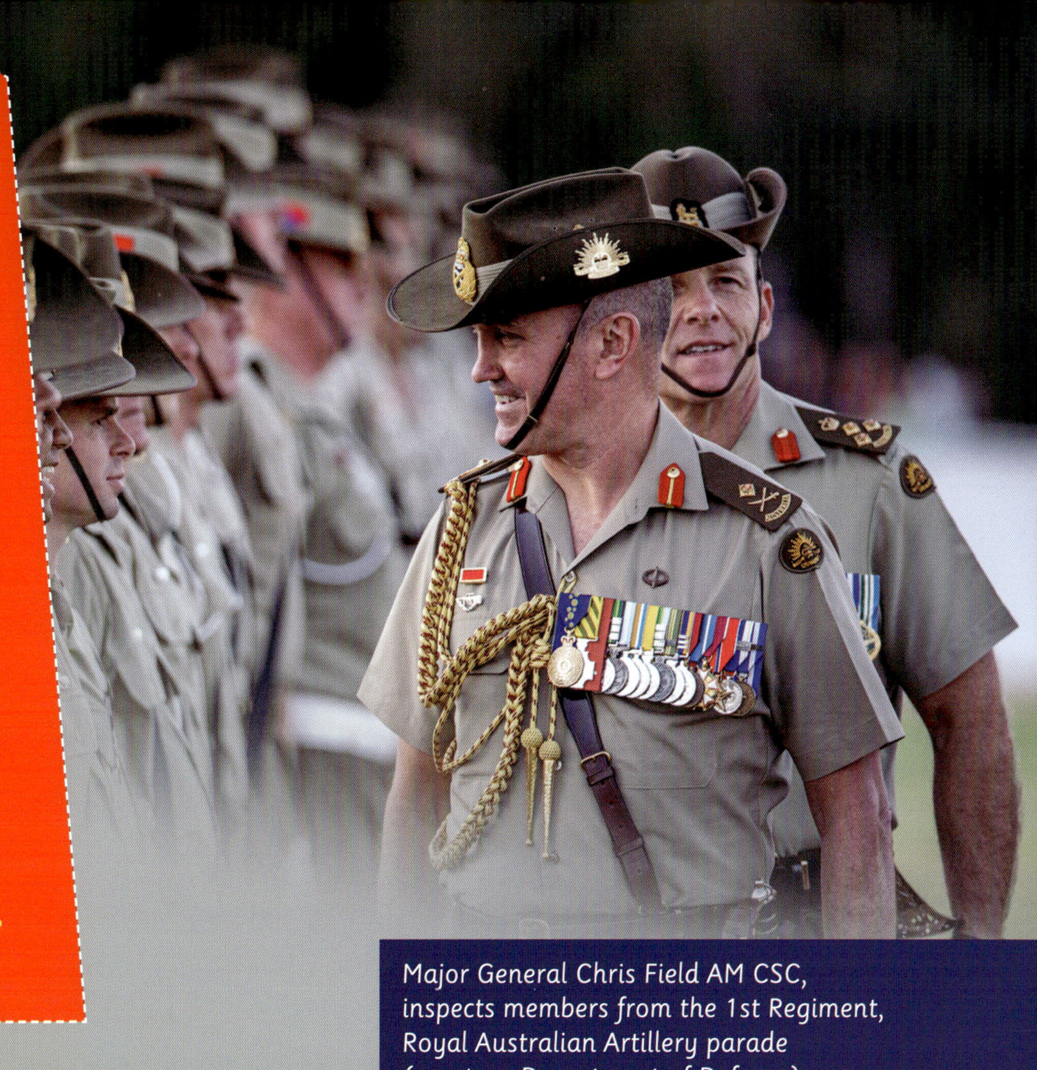

Major General Chris Field AM CSC, inspects members from the 1st Regiment, Royal Australian Artillery parade (courtesy Department of Defence).

Inspections

An inspecting officer or a **dignitary,** like the Governor-General, Prime Minister or Chief of the Defence Force, might perform an inspection of the Guard of Honour. **Servicemen and women** line up and the dignitary walks along the lines to inspect the service personnel. The ceremony dates to the 17th century and a time of war in England. King Charles II was unsure if some strange troops he encountered were on his side. The troops formed up along the road for the king's inspection. He studied each of the men's faces to assess their character and readiness to fight for him.

Military Drills

All members of the ADF are taught special marches and movements called military drills which are performed on parades. Aside from being ceremonial and creating a feeling of unity, drill movements teach self-discipline, teamwork, alertness and obedience, qualities which assist service personnel to carry out orders when under pressure.

The tradition of parades and drills can even be found in ancient Greek warfare with evidence of soldiers moving in tight formations rather than independently. In 1788, the British Army created a manual for the teaching of eighteen drill movements which were designed to help move troops in formation around a battlefield. Each year a reviewing general would inspect the various regiments as they performed the drills to decide whether they were ready for battle. The tradition of reviewing drill movements continues today.

A Police Command Superintendent halts the crew of the HMAS *Watson*, (courtesy Navy News).

In the past, the drills learnt on the parade ground were important for success on a battlefield. The parade ground's value in training and discipline means that it should not be crossed or used as a shortcut. The paths around the parade grounds should be used instead.

Maryborough Freedom of Entry Scroll

Freedom of Entry

Freedom of Entry (sometimes called Freedom of the City) is one of the oldest and highest accolades a city, town or region can give to a military unit. The tradition can be traced to Roman and medieval times when cities were behind walls. Armed troops were not allowed to enter a city with their weapons. Military units who were considered trustworthy could enter and the gates were opened for them even when they were armed. Today it is a special honour usually given to a unit that has a close association with the city. The unit parades through the city before being inspected by the Lord Mayor or other city official. A scroll granting Freedom of Entry is presented to the troops who then parade through the city with their weapons.

DID YOU KNOW?

In the Army, the Regimental Sergeant Major carries a pace stick. The stick has been used for centuries in the British and Commonwealth armies to measure the distance between field artillery guns. It was also used to measure the length of the pace of marching troops, hence its name — the pace stick. Pace sticks belonging to artillery regiments are black while others are timber. In the RAAF, the Warrant Officer carries a rosewood pace stick.

Freedom of Entry Parade of HMAS Watson at Woollahra on 25 May 2019 (courtesy Navy News).

Military Drill (courtesy Department of Defence).

Members of RAAF march past the Governor-General of Australia 2019 (courtesy Department of Defence).

Why do members of the ADF turn their heads towards important people when they are marching in a parade?

In marches and parades, the marching servicemen and women might turn their head and look at an inspecting officer or important person as they march by. They are ordered to turn 'eyes right' or 'eyes left'. This is a sign of equality as they are permitted to look at the important person. In medieval times, bondmen (often slaves) had to look at the ground to avoid the eyes of a knight.

Salutes

Saluting is a tradition that dates to ancient times. If a group of soldiers approached another group, or even if naval vessels at sea were in sight, it was a good idea to determine whether they were friendly or hostile! A salute is a greeting, a sign of friendship and respect. It is also a sign of loyalty and respect for the Service to which the member belongs. It varies from the simple hand salute as a personal greeting, to the firing of guns, called a gun or artillery salute.

A Regimental Sergeant Major carrying a pace stick (courtesy Department of Defence).

The Hand Salute

The tradition of saluting by raising a hand may have begun in medieval times when friendly knights would flip their visors on their helmets back to greet one another or take off their helmets. It was sometimes awkward to do that, so they would raise their right hand to their head as a greeting, while their left hand remained holding the reins of their horse. It was considered friendly as it took their right hand away from their sword. The origin may even date further with Stone Age paintings depicting a type of salute. Service personnel salute a superior officer as an acknowledgment of the officer's rank and the officer returns the salute.

DID YOU KNOW?

Army and RAAF personnel salute with the right hand facing outward, while sailors salute with their hand facing down. It is thought this originated as sailors tended to have dirty hands from the work they did on board their ship. To salute with a dirty hand was considered rude. There is a story, which may or may not be true, that Queen Victoria, the Queen of Great Britain and Ireland from 1837 to 1901, was once saluted by a sailor with a grimy palm. She decreed that in future all sailors should salute with their hand facing down!

Some customs and traditions seem silly, but they give guidance to processes and procedures.

Brad Dunn, RSM (Retired)

Chief of Navy, the Chief of Army and the Chief of Air Force salute at a Remembrance Day Service at the Australian War Memorial, Canberra, 2019 (courtesy Department of Defence).

Piping the Side

The custom of Piping the Side is a naval salute which is part of what is known as the Gangway Ceremonial. It dates from the days when a ship's captain needed to report to the senior officer's flagship at sea. When the sea was too rough to use a gangway, a visiting captain would be hoisted on board using a Bosun's chair. The orders were made using the Boatswain's Call. The pipe could be heard above the sound of the ocean or bad weather. Today, dignitaries will be saluted by 'Piping the Side' as they arrive on board, and as they depart the ship.

DID YOU KNOW?

The quarterdeck is an important part of a naval ship. Traditionally it was the raised deck behind the main mast where the captain or master commanded the ship and where ceremonies were held. The ship's colours (its flag) were also kept there. In times past, the quarterdeck was where a shrine or crucifix would be placed. Saluting the shrine or crucifix was a religious duty and thought to bring good luck for the journey. In today's modern ships, a quarterdeck is not a specific deck, but an area chosen for ceremonies. Sailors salute the quarterdeck and the officer of the day when boarding or leaving naval vessels.

FAST FACT!

The senior officer always boards the ship last and leaves first!

DID YOU KNOW?

Not all customs are official! Crossing the Line is an unofficial ceremony performed on ships to recognise those on board who are crossing the equator for the first time. It may date to ancient times when sailors performed a religious ceremony to ask the gods of the sea to keep them safe. There are records of Captain Cook ordering a dunking ceremony of those who were crossing the equator for the first time while on board the HMS *Endeavour* in 1768. The dogs and cats were also dunked! Today, there are rules that keep sailors safe in a ceremony involving being dunked in seawater. King Neptune, another sailor dressed in costume, orders the dunking and awards the new sailors as he accepts them as one of his 'shellbacks'. Crossing the Line ceremonies are often held on holiday cruise ships as a form of entertainment.

FAST FACT

The 'heads' was the name given to that part of a sailing ship of the past which was used by the crew as their toilet. The heads were floored with gratings, and open to the sea, so that the sea could help wash the floor down. Washing the heads was frequently used as a punishment for sailors who were in trouble! Sailors today still call the toilets 'the heads'.

Piping the Side (courtesy Department of Defence).

Rifle and Artillery (Gun) Salutes

The custom of firing weapons to salute royalty and high-ranking officers began in naval traditions of the 14th century. When a ship was approaching a port, or a friendly ship, all the cannons on board would be fired at once to show they were empty and no threat. In those days it took some time to reload a cannon. The ship was trusting that the other ship or people in the port would not open fire. This custom became a way of greeting and showing respect to important people. The salute developed to each gun firing one after the other. The number of guns fired depends on the person's importance, for example the Queen receives a 21-gun salute while an Admiral, General or Air Marshal receives a 17-gun salute.

DID YOU KNOW?

Before the arrival of planes and helicopters, it was common for a sailor to be buried at sea. The body was wrapped in a canvas cover and stitched with a weight at his feet. The last stich was sewn through the nose, possibly to stop the body from slipping out of the canvas and to check the person had died. A national flag was draped over the body and a service held. The body was then slipped from under the flag and into the ocean.

A Gun Salute on Australia Day, Darwin 2011 (courtesy Department of Defence).

DID YOU KNOW?

Swords and rifles are used in salutes. Knights once kissed the hilt (handle) of the sword before going into battle. The hilt was considered to represent a Christian cross. Swords today are ceremonial and not used as weapons. Guns are also used in the Rifle Butt Salute or Present Arms. Service personnel hold their weapons at arm's length and then in a position over their right shoulder so it can't be used. They salute by passing their left hand over the rifle at waist height. Rifles and swords are also held in front of the body as a sign that they are no threat. Presenting Arms dates to the 17th century and a time of war in England when the monarchy was overthrown. King Charles II packed his bags and went to Europe. When he returned nine years later, soldiers of a regiment held up their weapons in a harmless position to show King Charles II that they were loyal and no threat to him!

FAST FACT

Three rifle volleys can be fired at the funeral service of an ADF member. It is a gesture of respect and remembrance.

A Gun Salute (courtesy Department of Defence).

FAST FACT

There are six different types of swords that soldiers of the Australian Army might carry.

Ceremonial swords have amazing histories. The curved Mameluke sword can be traced to the Mamluk warriors of 16th century-Egypt, while the two-handed Claymore was a Scottish weapon from the 15th century.

The Mameluke sword (courtesy Major General Mick Slater DSC, AM, CSC).

A flypast at a commemorative event in Hobart 2019 (courtesy Department of Defence).

Why do planes sometimes fly overhead at an Anzac Day or Remembrance Day ceremony?

A flypast is an aerial salute used at commemorative services and ceremonies by air forces all over the world. Planes fly in close formation and close to the ground as a sign of respect. Flying in this way, the crew are placing themselves where they could be fired at from the ground. A flypast is also used to entertain people at air shows.

A Lieutenant General presents a sword of honour to a graduating officer, 2010 (courtesy Department of Defence).

Receiving my wings eclipsed many major events in my life. It was a mountain to climb, something I never thought I would achieve, but I did ... you nearly feel invincible ...

Peter Clements, Flight Lieutenant and former Roulettes pilot

Sometimes sporting clubs and other organisations have their own drills. Do you know of any?

DID YOU KNOW?

There is a special aerial salute called the Missing Man Formation, which can be used at a Service funeral. The flypast formation is missing one plane. Alternatively, an aircraft will pull away from the others and climb steeply into the sky as the others fly ahead. This formation may have begun in World War I, but the first official record of it dates to the death of King George V in 1936.

A Missing Man Formation (courtesy Department of Defence).

The Roulettes complete a flying display in Melbourne, 2018 (courtesy Department of Defence).

FAST FACT

The Royal Australian Air Force Roulettes are an aerobatic display team which fly at low level and perform various manoeuvres which are based on the skills they learn as pilots in the RAAF. Their first public display was at RAAF Base Point Cook, Victoria, in 1970.

Chapter 7

FLAGS, STANDARDS, GUIDONS, COLOURS, BANNERS & PENDANTS

The Australian National Flag

Australia's flag is an important **symbol** which represents our history, identifies us as Australian and encourages us to feel proud of our nation.

The Australian National Flag was introduced in 1901 and combines the British flag with Australian symbols. It has been modified several times since then. The Union Flag or **Union Jack** is in the upper corner to show Australia's link with the United Kingdom. The Southern Cross symbolises the great southern land while the seven-pointed star represents the six states of Federation and the Commonwealth territories.

The Australian National Flag is the **ensign** of the Australian Army which has the ceremonial role as protector of the flag. The Navy and Air Force have their own separate ensigns as does the combined ADF.

Australian National Flag.

Flags, or ensigns as they are also known, are significant to the ADF. There are many different types and each one is symbolic and has a specific meaning.

The Australian White Ensign is the ensign of the Royal Australian Navy. It was first used in 1967, before then the white ensign of the Royal Navy was used.

Australian Defence Force Ensign – the dark blue stripe represents the Navy, red represents the Army and light blue is the Air Force. – The ADF emblem is in the centre of the flag.

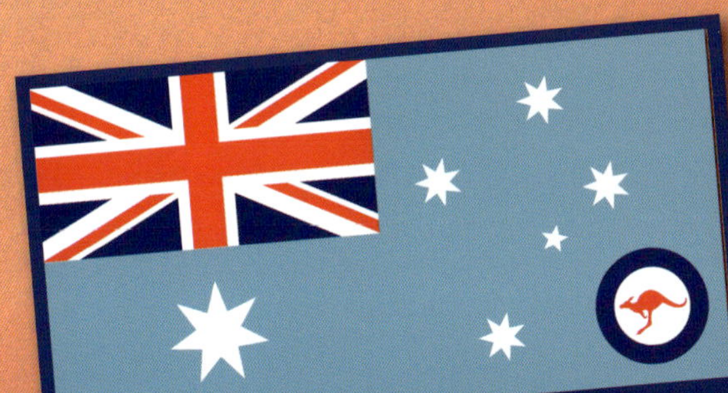

Royal Australian Air Force Ensign – the RAAF ensign was approved by King George VI in 1948 with light blue symbolising the sky. The British roundel in the bottom fly corner was changed to include a kangaroo in 1982.

Why is the Australian Ensign sometimes red?

The Australian Red Ensign is used for merchant ships that are registered in Australia, not RAN ships!

DID YOU KNOW?

On a Royal Australian Navy ship the Australian National Flag (ANF) is flown from the bow. Sailors refer to the ANF as the 'Jack'. The Australian White Ensign (AWE) is flown from the stern of a ship. Commissioned Navy ships also fly a long, thin flag called a Commissioning Pendant at the masthead, where it remains for the whole of the ship's life.

The Australian Aboriginal Flag

The Australian Aboriginal Flag was first raised on National Aborigines' Day on 12 July 1971. Today it is flown at many memorials and Government facilities across Australia. Black symbolises Aboriginal people, the earth and the colour of ochre used in Aboriginal ceremonies is represented by red and the yellow circle symbolises the sun as the constant renewer of life.

The Torres Strait Islander Flag

The Torres Strait Islander flag was first raised in 1992 at the Torres Strait Islands Cultural Festival. The green stripes represent the land, the blue represents the sea and the black represents the people. The symbol in the centre is a dancer's headdress called a 'dari'. Underneath the 'dari' is a five-pointed star with each point representing the five island groups of the Torres Strait. The colour white represents peace.

Visitors have placed Australian National Flags and Australian Aboriginal Flags on a memorial site of a WWI battle at Pozières, France.

A standard of days past.

The Torres Strait Islander Flag being raised, 2016 (courtesy Department of Defence).

Where do you see flags flying in your daily life?

DID YOU KNOW?

A Service person in uniform must salute a vehicle that is flying a distinguishing flag such as a car carrying the Prime Minister or a General.

Standards, Guidons, Colours and Banners

Standards, guidons, colours and banners are all types of flags which are displayed and carried in ceremonial parades by units of the ADF, or by high-ranking officers. They are designed to represent a unit and its history. Royalty and senior defence personnel can display a personal flag or a pennant which is flown when travelling or in residence.

FAST FACT

Symbols have been carried into battle for centuries, including in Roman times. The Eagle Standards of the Roman Legions are the most famous and were a pole with the figure of an eagle attached to the top. The eagle represented power and courage.

Why is there a type of flag called a colour?

The Regimental Colours of the 41st Battalion, AIF which shows the battle honours of WWI.

The colour is a flag carried into battles since ancient times to provide a point where the fighting forces would gather. While it was intact, there was hope, even after a commander had been wounded or killed. The use of the word 'colours' for this type of flag can be traced back to 1588. Later, at the start of the 17th century, when the British Army adopted a system of regiments, the King ordered that each regiment be given a colour. In a parade, the colours are carried with great care by a junior officer who is protected by the 'colour party'. Members of the colour party always wear white gloves because the cloth of the colour should not be touched by bare hands. Service personnel never turn their back on any colour, even those from other countries. Colours are passed on over time, are respected and proudly protected. They are lowered only to show respect, courtesy, mourning or surrender.

Standards

A standard is square in shape and one of the largest types of flags flown in armies in the Middle Ages. A standard was designed to stand in one place rather than be carried into battle, hence its name 'standard'. In medieval times, the nobility or high-ranking knights carried a standard, while less important knights carried a guidon (pronounced gee-on) which has one end shaped like the tail of a swallow. Today, a standard can be awarded to a unit by a monarch and is the most senior of the flags.

An armoured vehicle displays the Standard during a parade, 2019 (courtesy Department of Defence).

DID YOU KNOW?

During the 13th century, the nobility went into battle with most of their body and horse covered in protective armour. Badges and crests were used on their equipment for identification, including on banners and pendants. The symbols used were passed on in families or armies and became known as heraldic symbols - symbols of identification that were inherited! Regimental Colours can be traced to the use of these banners.

A Squadron Standard is presented to a RAAF Squadron by the Governor-General of Australia, Amberley, 2019 (courtesy Department of Defence).

Battle Honours

A 'Battle Honour' recognises an outstanding achievement of a unit under combat and links that achievement to where and when it happened. A unit's battle honours represent important past events that are often commemorated by those serving in the current unit. In the Army, a Battle Honour is embroidered on the unit's own special flag called the Colours. RAAF battle honours are embroidered on a type of flag called the Squadron Standard. The Battle Honours of ships of the RAN and their crews are also recorded on a board and placed in a prominent position on the ship, usually on both sides of the navigation bridge.

A banner displaying the battle honours of HMAS *Sydney* (courtesy Department of Defence).

Australian Army soldiers complete a Lowering of Colours Salute at the First Australian Division Memorial, Pozieres, France, 2016 (courtesy Department of Defence).

DID YOU KNOW?

The Navy has a special flag ceremony known as the Colours, Sunset and Ceremonial Sunset. The Australian White Ensign and Australian National Flag are hoisted at 8.00 am and lowered at sunset at naval bases, or on board ships when they are in port, or at anchorage. The ship's bell is rung eight times and the Boatswain's Call is piped. At sunset a similar ceremony occurs, and the flags are lowered.

The Ceremonial Sunset is used on special occasions and includes music, drums and a volley of shots fired as a salute. 'Beat to Quarters' is played on the drums, a tradition dating back to when sailors were called to action stations ready for battle by the beat of a drum. Today it honours the courage and sacrifice of sailors.

Why is a flag sometimes lowered to half-mast?

A flag is lowered to half-mast as a sign of remembrance and respect for those who have lost their lives. It is thought that the tradition began as an old naval custom in the early 1600s. A captain in the Royal Navy had been killed and his ship returned to port with its ensign at half-mast to show respect. Later, in 1660, the Royal Navy was ordered to fly its flags at half-mast on the anniversary of the death of King Charles I who was executed during the civil war in England. Another belief is that the flying of a flag at half-mast allows for an 'invisible flag of death' to fly at the top.

A flag at half-mast is always hoisted to the top of the mast before being lowered.

Lowering of Colours Salute

Regimental colours are lowered and are then held horizontal. This is one of the highest displays of respect. This custom dates back to 1786.

What is a flagship?

A flagship is the lead ship in a fleet of vessels and is used by the officer commanding the whole fleet, or smaller group of ships called a **flotilla**. It flies the officer's special flag and is usually the best known, fastest, most capable, or most heavily armed vessel in the fleet.

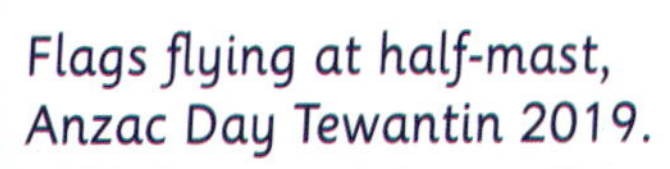

Flags flying at half-mast, Anzac Day Tewantin 2019.

Chapter 8

BADGES, AWARDS AND HONOURS

Like flags, the badges, symbols, awards and honours of the Australian Defence Force create pride in its members and reinforce its history, along with its customs and traditions.

There are many badge designs used to identify the unique abilities of the ADF's joint Service units. The badges are protected by law and designed within guidelines and rules about colours, symbols and the use of animals and objects. The design of a badge may connect the unit to its role, location or the history and past achievements of the unit.

The Australian Defence Force Emblem

The ADF Emblem is the official joint Service emblem of the Australian Defence Force. The ADF Emblem takes prominence and priority over the single Service emblems when more than one Service is represented.

The ADF Emblem

Today's RAN badge

The original badge of RAN

Royal Australian Navy Badge

The Royal Australian Navy badge has had several changes since it was officially adopted in 1949. The original design had a rope surrounding the badge which was knotted at the base, an anchor and chain and four dots placed between the Federation Star and the words 'Royal Australian Navy'. The crown was originally the Tudor Crown. In 1953 Queen Elizabeth became our monarch. She requested that the design be changed to that of the crown used at her coronation ceremony, called the St Edward's Crown. The new design was first used in 1957. Several more changes have been made over the years, with the current badge adopted in 2002.

The Rising Sun Badge

The Rising Sun Badge is one of Australia's most valued and respected emblems that marks an Australian soldier and the Anzac spirit. It is officially called the Australian Army Badge. The metal badge is worn on the upturned brim of a slouch hat. Today it is also worn as a cloth badge on a soldier's uniform, positioned on the left upper sleeve. It has changed over time and was in use before World War I.

Although the Rising Sun symbol had previously been used by colonial military regiments, it is accepted that the first version of the badge was chosen after federation in February, 1902. It was first worn by Australian forces serving in South Africa during the Boer War (1899-1902). The design of the badge is thought to have been that of a British officer, Major General Sir Edward Hutton, the Commander-in-Chief of the Australian troops. Hutton may have been inspired by a gift he had received of a 'trophy of arms' made from mounted swords and bayonets arranged in a semi-circle around the crown, which looks like a rising sun (The Hutton Trophy). However, the origins of the badge are still disputed. There are several accounts of its design which involve other people and influences, including the rising sun logo used on jam tins and bottles by Hoadley's jam producers!

Since 1902, there have been several designs, but the distinctive shape of the Rising Sun Badge remained. It has has become a symbol of the spirit of Anzac.

The Evolution of the Rising Sun Badge
(Australian Army Badge)

The Hutton Trophy

The First Pattern - February 1902

The Second Pattern - April 1902

The Third Pattern - May 1904

The Fourth Pattern - 1949

The Fifth Pattern - 1954

The Sixth Pattern - 1969

The Seventh Pattern - 1991

Does your school or sports club have a badge?

Royal Australian Air Force Badge

The Royal Australian Air Force badge features a crown mounted on a circle with the Australian wedge-tailed eagle. The original design was accepted in 1939 and was in use until 1957. It features the RAAF motto in Latin, *Per Ardua Ad Astra*, 'Through adversity to the stars'. Originally the crown was in the shape of a Tudor Crown, or the King's Crown. Like the RAN badge, the design was changed to the St Edward's Crown in 1957.

The RAAF Badge of today features the St Edward's Crown or, as it is commonly called, the Queen's Crown. (courtesy Department of Defence).

The RAAF Badge of 1939-1957 which featured the King's Crown (courtesy Department of Defence).

DID YOU KNOW?

The eagle has been a symbol used on the uniforms, badges and crests of many air services around the world, including the RAAF. An eagle was first used by the British Royal Naval Air Service (RNAS) in World War I. Later there was some debate over whether the bird was an albatross rather than an eagle. The problem was settled when an order from the Admiralty in June 1914 was uncovered which stated: 'The badge of an eagle will be worn by members of the RNAS at the top of the left sleeve.' The RAAF uses the wedge-tailed eagle which is the biggest bird of prey in Australia.

DID YOU KNOW?

Sometimes the badges worn by military personnel are not official. In the past, RAAF pilots might receive a badge if they survived when their planes were lost in enemy action. They included the Caterpillar Pin for surviving enemy action and baling out using a parachute made of silk, or a Winged Boot for returning to their bases from behind enemy lines.

The Caterpillar Pin awarded to Max's great-grandfather, RAAF Warrant Officer George Henry Pringle, a World War II wireless operator whose aircraft was lost over Germany on 22 May 1942. George was the only crew member to survive after parachuting to safety. He was captured and became a prisoner of war. The red eyes of the caterpillar indicate that George actually jumped from a burning aircraft and makes the award even more valuable (courtesy Jacinta Leo).

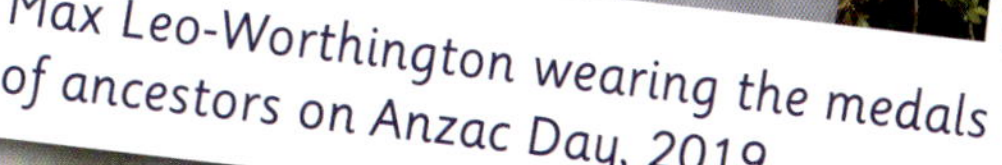

Max Leo-Worthington wearing the medals of ancestors on Anzac Day, 2019.

I feel extraordinary to step in the footsteps of my great-grandfather and great-great uncles. I feel very proud.

Max Leo-Worthington

This wedge-tailed eagle is called Trooper Courage and is the mascot of the 2nd Cavalry Regiment based in Townsville (courtesy Department of Defence).

The Royal Australian Air Force Roundel

The RAAF roundel (circular disc) is an emblem used on all RAAF planes and equipment which identifies them as Australian. The RAAF initially adopted the Royal Air Force's red, white and blue roundel. However, this has an inner red circle that resembled the symbol of the Japanese forces. A RAAF plane was mistaken for a Japanese aircraft by the United States Navy in World War II and attacked. After that, the red inner circle was removed but reintroduced after the war. In 1956, the current version was adopted with a white inner circle and a red kangaroo surrounded by a royal blue circle. The 'leaping kangaroo' faces left, except when used on aircraft or vehicles when the kangaroo always faces in the direction of forward travel.

A RAAF aircraft of the 1920's - the D.H.50A - with the roundel of Britain's Royal Air Force (courtesy RAAF Museum).

RAAF Roundel.

DID YOU KNOW?

Pilots who have completed their training, passed certain tests and flown for eighteen months are awarded a special badge called the Flying Badge or pilots' 'wings'. In 1913, when military aviation had only just begun, King George V approved the first 'wings' design for the Royal Flying Corps, which featured the wings of a bird called a swift. The badge, or brevet, was stitched onto the left breast of a pilot's jacket. The original design was modified for the RAAF.

The 'wings' of a World War II RAAF pilot (courtesy RAAF)

FAST FACT!

The Army has roundels as well. Army Aviation uses the symbol of a black kangaroo, while armoured sections use a red one on various types of transport. The symbol of the leaping kangaroo can even be found on warships!

HMAS *Melbourne*, 2019 (courtesy Department of Defence).

Ribbons and medals worn by a descendant of veteran (courtesy of St Andrew's Anglican College).

DID YOU KNOW?

The coloured stripes of ribbons attached to medals depend on the campaign for which the medal was awarded and which Services were involved in that campaign. Usually a navy blue stripe represents the Navy, the Army stripe is red, and RAAF is light blue. Other colours on the ribbon show where the campaign was located e.g. a jungle might be green, the desert a sand colour, or the ocean might be blue.

Medals and Honours

For centuries, kings, queens and governments have rewarded units and individuals for outstanding service. Members of the ADF are awarded medals for their service during times of conflict, or outstanding service when not at war. They can also receive medals which honour acts of bravery or leadership during battle. Coloured ribbons are attached to the medal and there are rules about the order in which the medals are positioned. Servicemen and women wear their own medals on their left side over their heart.

Victoria Cross for Australia

The Victoria Cross for Australia is the highest gallantry award in Australia. It is awarded for conspicuous gallantry, acts of valour or self-sacrifice, or displays of extreme devotion to duty in the face of the enemy. The Victoria Cross was created in 1856 during the reign of Queen Victoria. From 1975, Australia developed its own system of awards and honours rather than using the British system. The Victoria Cross was renamed the Victoria Cross for Australia by Queen Elizabeth II in 1991. It is the same design and its awarding must still be approved by the Queen.

Former Australian soldier Keith Payne, VC AM wearing his Service medals which includes the Victoria Cross awarded for action in 1969 during the Vietnam War (courtesy Department of Defence).

Australian Gallantry Decorations

Gallantry decorations are awarded for acts of bravery in warlike conditions which are above that normally expected of people in similar situations. They can only be awarded to ADF members.

The Australian Gallantry Decorations are (starting with the highest):

Victoria Cross for Australia (VC)

Star of Gallantry (SG)

Medal for Gallantry (MG)

Commendation for Gallantry

Commonwealth Coat of Arms

Centuries ago, kings and queens, lords and knights would rally their troops to war by calling 'to arms, to arms'. They proudly wore the symbols or 'arms' of their families on tunics over their armour to represent their courage and motivate the troops. Monarchs granted knights special permission to wear their own coat of arms as a reward for their courage and loyalty. Later, other people, towns, organisations and even countries were granted their own coat of arms. Australia's first national coat of arms was granted by King Edward VII in 1908. It was altered in 1912 by King George V to include the symbols of the states and the floral emblem, the Golden Wattle.

The Australian Service Medal 1945–1975 – the *Commonwealth Coat of Arms* is on one side and the Federation Star is on the other.

School students marching, Anzac Day, Tewantin, 2019.

FAST FACT

Individuals who receive the same award more than once do not receive another medal. Instead they receive a bar that clasps to the ribbon.

Australian Bravery Decorations

These decorations can be awarded to both ADF members and civilians.

The Australian Bravery Decorations are (starting with the highest):

- Cross of Valour (CV)
- Star of Courage (SC)
- Bravery Medal (BM)
- Commendation for Brave Conduct

Nursing Service Cross

The Nursing Service Cross is awarded for outstanding devotion and competency in the performance of nursing duties under warlike or non-warlike conditions.

Nursing Service Cross

Distinguished Service Cross

Distinguished Service Medal

Commendation for Distinguished Service

Distinguished Service Decorations

Distinguished Service Decorations may be awarded to ADF members or other persons for distinguished command, leadership or performance of duties under warlike conditions.

On what side of the chest do you wear the medals of a relative?

On days such as Anzac Day, family members sometimes wear the medals of service personnel who lost their lives while serving, or who have passed away. The medals should be worn on the right side of the chest when they are not your own. Service personnel wear their own medals on their left side over their hearts.

Conspicuous Service Decorations

The Conspicuous Service Cross and Conspicuous Service Medal were created in 1989 to acknowledge outstanding achievement and performance of duty when not at war.

Conspicuous Service Cross

Conspicuous Service Medal

It feels special to march with Pop's medals, and Dad's.

Hannah and Charli Crooks

Why do people choose to wear an ancestor's medals on Anzac Day and Remembrance Day? Have you ever worn an ancestor's medals?

Hannah Crooks wearing replicas of her father's medals and Charli Crooks wearing replicas of her grandfather's medals, Anzac Day, Tewantin, 2019.

Chapter 9

RANK AND NAMES

The Navy, Army and Air Force all have different ways in which they are structured and different rank systems. A rank is determined by the person's skill level, the job they do, their qualifications and the courses they have completed. Different badges and symbols are worn on uniforms which depict the rank of a member of the ADF.

DID YOU KNOW?

The word 'soldier' comes from Roman times when soldiers were paid in salt which they could trade for goods they needed. Eventually salt was replaced by money which was called 'salt money'. In France this payment was known as 'solde' and paid with a coin known as the 'sol'. The word 'solde' was used to describe a person as well. It became part of the English language and is the origin of the word 'soldier'.

HMAS *Sydney I.*

HMAS *Sydney II.*

Crew members of HMAS *Ballarat* returning to Australia, July 2019 (courtesy Department of Defence).

Royal Australian Navy

Commissioned ships, submarines and bases of the RAN have a name beginning with HMAS. An identifying number, called a pennant number, is usually painted on both sides of the bow. Names are selected from Australian locations such as regions, cities, towns and rivers, names of First Australian tribes, or the names of distinguished sailors. Names are often passed down from a ship that is being retired to its replacement. HMAS *Sydney* was one of Australia's best-known ships and is named after the capital city of New South Wales. HMAS *Sydney* (I) was responsible for the capture of the German raider *Emden* in 1914 at the beginning of World War I. It was decommissioned in 1928. HMAS *Sydney* (II) was lost with all of its 645 crew members on 19 November 1941 after a battle with the German cruiser *Kormoran*.

Why do ships of the Royal Australian Navy have the letters HMAS in their name?

In 1911 all RAN ships became known as His Majesty's Australian Ships (HMAS) rather than His Majesty's Ships (HMS) which is used on the vessels of the Royal Navy. When the Queen became our head of state, the ships were referred to as Her Majesty's Australian Ships.

A precinct of the Gallipoli Barracks at Enoggera, Queensland is named after Lieutenant Colonel Vivian Bullwinkel who courageously served with the Australian Army Nursing Service in World War II. (courtesy Department of Defence).

What reasons might there be for naming a location or equipment after a person? What can you discover about Lieutenant Colonel Vivian Bullwinkel?

Army

Army bases and equipment might be named after campaigns, battles, personnel, or their location. Names are chosen to create historical links such as the naming of the Gallipoli Barracks in Brisbane, Queensland.

RAAF Aircraft numbering.

Royal Australian Air Force Aircraft

RAAF aircraft often have distinguishing **squadron** markings on them, a practice dating back to the first aeroplanes of World War I. The markings allowed pilots to identify friendly aeroplanes during combat. During World War II, the markings were usually letters painted on the side of the aircraft. The first two letters identified the squadron and the single letter on the other side of the roundel identified the actual aircraft. Today, squadron markings are based on the approved unit badge and usually placed on the tail of the aircraft. Some larger aircraft also have them on the body.

Since the RAAF was formed in 1921, a serial number was allocated to each aircraft. This system of numbering is still in use. The serial number begins with the letter A, followed by a number that identifies the aircraft type. Another number identifies the individual aircraft. Aircraft of the navy begin with the letter N.

The nose art of the Spitfire 457 on display at the Darwin Aviation Museum.

An RE8 ready for flight.

Why do some aircraft have pictures on their noses?

Pictures on aircraft are called nose art and often include animals. The RAAF 457 Spitfire Squadron painted the nose, teeth and jaws of the grey nurse shark and called itself the Grey Nurse Squadron.

A restored WWI RE8 aircraft at Point Cook in 2019 (photographer James Kightly)

DID YOU KNOW?

In World War I an aircraft called the RE8 was known to be unreliable and was nicknamed 'Harry Tate' after a popular comedian at the time whose name rhymed with RE8.

During World War II the RAAF used planes known as a Kittyhawk. Flight Lieutenant Bruce 'Buster' Brown named his regular plane 'Polly', after his girlfriend. In 1942 it was damaged several times in battles against Japanese planes known as Zeros. 'Polly' is displayed at the Australian War Memorial.

Chapter 10

UNIFORMS

The first known British military uniform dates from the 14th century. For centuries the uniforms, apart from colours and some decorations, were similar to normal clothing. In the 19th century they became extravagant, often brightly coloured and not very practical! The very first sailors and soldiers to arrive in Australia wore British uniforms of blue and red. Since then the uniforms have changed considerably, but the tradition of adding decorative pieces called **accoutrements** has remained.

The colourful uniforms of the colonial armies were later replaced by the khaki uniform which the first Anzacs wore. The slouch hat was worn and cloth regimental colour patches were stitched to the upper arm of a soldier's jacket. Khaki is still used in uniforms of the Army today.

The colour patches of the 38th Battalion.

DID YOU KNOW?

Australian soldiers wear colour patches to identify them as belonging to a unit. This tradition began during World War I when the patches of different shapes and colours were sewn to the sleeves of uniforms. Each patch had two colours, the bottom colour represented the parent brigade and the top was the soldier's battalion. In 1949, Australian soldiers stopped wearing patches. Being proud of their heritage, the Army reintroduced the tradition in 1987. The patches are worn on the right side of the puggaree on the slouch hat.

While soldiers originally wore a single uniform for all occasions, they were later issued with different types of uniforms, one for daily wear, another called a 'service' or 'battledress' and yet another that was a formal 'full-dress' uniform for parades and ceremonial occasions. The Navy and Air Force also developed different uniforms for certain purposes.

Uniforms used in ceremonies are adorned with accoutrements such as badges, medals and gold braid. Achievements in battle and rank will determine how decorative the wearer's uniform is!

Lieutenant Allan Marlow in 1918 with his slouch hat, Rising Sun Badges on his collar and hat, epaulettes with rank and the colour patch of the 38th Battalion on his shoulder. He is holding a cane or swagger stick. These date back to the 17th Century and the reign of King Charles I. In those days, junior officers carried swagger sticks to punish soldiers by striking them with the cane for minor offences!

Officers wearing full-dress uniform at a graduation parade at the Royal Military College – Duntroon, Canberra (courtesy Department of Defence).

A member of the 7th Australian Light Horse Regiment (7ALH) sewing new colour patches on his uniform in 1918 (AWM B00160).

Accoutrements

There are many different types of accoutrements or decorative pieces that are worn on the uniforms of the ADF, some of these had specific purposes in the past but have become tradition today. The wearing of accoutrements depends on rank and role and there are rules surrounding how they are worn.

Army Generals in full dress uniform.

FAST FACT!

An epaulette is an ornamental shoulder piece which varies according to rank. The name comes from the French word *épaule* which means 'shoulder'.

Aiguillettes

Flag Lieutenant to the Admiral Commanding the Australia Fleet, Max Hancock wearing an aiguillette in 1980 (courtesy Retired Admiral Max Hancock).

The aiguillette is worn by officers performing a specific support role or function for a senior officer such as an Admiral or other dignitary. It consists of braided loops that hang from the shoulder and end in metal points that look like pencils. There are several theories of the origin of aiguillettes. A common tale of its origin is that it represents the rope and pickets carried by a squire to tether the horse of a knight. Another thought is that it represents the pins used to fasten the shoulder protectors of a knight's armour to the chest plate. There again, it could represent a pencil that staff officers might attach to their clothing with a piece of string. Traditions evolve over time and often their origin will never be completely clear.

DID YOU KNOW?

Gorget patches are red tabs worn on the collar of coats and shirts of some senior personnel. The designs vary depending on rank. Gorget patches date back to the 14th Century and the times of suits of armour. Metal plates were used to protect the 'gorge' which is another name for the throat!

Major General Michael Jeffery AC CVO MC (Retd) was the Governor General of Australia from 2003-2008. In this photo taken in 2008 he is wearing his medals, badges and accoutrements which include the aiguillette, insignia on his shoulders which indicate his rank, gorget patches on his collar and a Sam Browne belt (courtesy Department of Defence).

Wearing the uniform of the Australian Army allows me to touch the face of my country's military heritage. It allows me to feel that I am echoing the noble tradition of those extraordinary men and women who wore this country's uniform in time of darkest conflict.

Cathy McCullagh, Australian Army

The Bandoleer dates back to the 17th Century and was a leather sash or belt with pockets on it that went over the shoulder. It was used for carrying powder charges for muskets. The word bandoleer comes from the Spanish word *banda* which means 'sash'. It is worn on the left shoulder under the epaulette.

DID YOU KNOW?

The lanyard is a cord worn by Australian soldiers which is looped over the right or left shoulder and tucked into the breast pocket. On which shoulder it is worn and its colour depends upon the unit, like battalion colours. Officers of the rank of colonel or above, along with Regimental Sergeants Major, do not wear lanyards. The origins of the wearing of the lanyard is uncertain. It may have been developed by the cavalry who attached a knife to the end of a cord, using it to cut ropes and as a hoof pick, while members of the artillery may have attached tools to a lanyard. The British Army officially mentions it in a guide on uniforms written in 1900 as a silk cord with a whistle attached. Australian soldiers also wore the lanyard with a clasp knife attached to it. Today the lanyard is worn with both ceremonial and work dress, but is not part of all uniforms.

Think about people in your community who wear a uniform. Do they wear any accoutrements which are similar to that of members of the Australian Defence Force?

FAST FACT

In the days when sailors had to supply their own clothing, they were occasionally given time off work to make and mend their clothes. Today, the Navy still uses the term to 'make and mend' to give the crew an afternoon holiday.

Are there times when you wear a uniform? Why? What is its purpose?

Airmen in the 'Cavalry of the Clouds' uniform in the 1920's (RAAF Museum).

Royal Australian Air Force – Shades of Blue

During World War I, the uniforms of the Australian Flying Corps were similar to those of the rest of the AIF. The 'wings' of the AFC were worn on the left breast, while an AFC colour patch and Rising Sun Badges were also worn. The colour blue was chosen for RAAF uniforms in 1922. The British Royal Air Force wanted Australia to have a grey uniform but Wing Commander (later Air Marshal) Sir Richard Williams preferred a dark blue of a shade that was different to that of the Navy. He visited the Commonwealth Woollen Mills at Geelong where he watched natural wool being dipped into indigo dye for naval uniforms. To create navy, the wool was dipped into five different machines. On the fourth dip Sir Richard found the right colour — a navy blue but one dip, or one shade lighter than that of the Navy.

Camouflage

Today, members of the ADF often wear a uniform that uses a camouflage pattern known as a Disruptive Pattern Camouflage Uniform. The Army patterns and colours of browns and greens were chosen based on the colours of the Australian landscape for camouflage purposes. The RAAF uses blue colours, while the Navy has greys and greens. The naval camouflage uniform has a reflective tape on the arm which assists visibility in low light. If a crew member falls overboard the sailor can easily be seen in the water.

Crew on board HMAS *Success* wearing the camouflage uniform with reflective tape (courtesy Navy News).

If you wear a uniform is there a reason it is a particular colour?

Why do some Australian soldiers wear kilts?

Kilts are a traditional form of dress worn by the people of Scotland. Many Scottish people came to Australia in the early years of settlement. The armies of the separate colonies had Scottish regiments. These regiments were the foundation for the Scottish regiments we see today which continue to wear kilts as part of their ceremonial uniform.

Kilted soldiers on parade in Sydney (courtesy Department of Defence).

Why do Australian soldiers wear a hat with the brim turned up?

The Slouch Hat is a national symbol worn by members of the Army. It is also known in the Army as the Hat Khaki Fur Felt and is made of rabbit or wool felt. The Slouch Hat was first worn by the troops of the Victorian Mounted Rifles in the 1880s and in other states of Australia by 1890. The brim was turned up to allow drill movements without rifles being caught in soldiers' hats. The Slouch Hat became a famous symbol of World War I soldiers and has been worn by Australian soldiers ever since. Today, members of the Army wear the brim looped up on the left side during ceremonies. The Rising Sun Badge is attached to the upturned brim.

DID YOU KNOW?
A cloth band called a puggaree is worn around the hat. The puggaree has had several designs over the years. There are variations, but the current puggaree is usually light khaki and has seven pleats, one for each state and one for the Australian territories. The colour patch of the soldier's unit is sewn on the right side of the puggaree. RAAF personnel also have a similar hat but do not wear it with the brim turned up.

Slouch Hat

Soldiers of a Light Horse Regiment wearing slouch hats with plumes, bandoleers and lanyards. They are also carrying lances which were an important weapon in the past for mounted soldiers and knights. Today, lances are only carried on ceremonial parades. The pennant of the unit is attached to the end. (courtesy Department of Defence).

Why do some soldiers wear feathers in their hat?

Australian soldiers first wore emu plumes in their slouch hats in 1891 when they were serving during the shearers' strike in Queensland. In a playful sporting challenge, the soldiers from the Gympie Squadron rode their horses alongside emus and plucked feathers to wear in their hats. In 1914, all Queensland Light Horsemen wore the plume. Permission was given to every member of the Australian Light Horse to wear the plumes in 1915. During World War I, Australian soldiers would jokingly tell soldiers from other countries that the emu plumes were kangaroo feathers. Today, members of the Royal Australian Armoured Corps continue to wear emu plumes in their hats.

Why are the shoes of sailors, soldiers and airmen and women so shiny?

Service personnel care for their uniforms with great pride, including their shoes! Today's dress uniform shoes are a naturally shiny patent leather that is polished until it gleams. In the past a Service person may have been issued with a pair of boots for wearing in the bush and a pair for parade which had to be 'spit polished' using nugget and spit, and lots of polishing! Stories have it that shoes had to be as reflective as a mirror so you could look into them when you shaved!

Officers wearing Sam Browne Belts, Le Havre, France, Armistice Day 1918.

DID YOU KNOW?

Army officers wear a wide leather belt supported by a strap fastened on the left side of the belt and passing over the right shoulder. It is usually brown, although the armoured, aviation and nursing corps wear black. This tradition began in the 19th century. General Sir Sam Browne of the British Indian Army had lost his left arm which made it difficult for him to use his sword. He needed his left hand to steady the scabbard as he drew out the sword with his right hand. He came up with idea of the belt design to hold the scabbard steady. He attached a holster on his right hip for a pistol and a binocular case with a neck strap. Other officers liked the Sam Browne belt and it soon became part of the standard uniform, eventually spreading to defence and policing organisations all over the world.

The Sam Browne Belt.

DID YOU KNOW?

The Royal Navy lacked a standard uniform up until the middle of the 18th century. A group of naval officers asked King George II to declare a standard form of dress. The officers enticed a Duchess to wear an outfit of dark blue with a white trim while riding where the King would see her. The King liked her outfit and declared the colours suitable for the Royal Navy!

A Sailor wearing the blue jean collar.

Sailors are often called 'Jack'. In the days of sail, the sailors wore pigtails which were usually kept in place by the tar used on board the ships. They became known as 'Jack Tar', later shortened to 'Jack'.

Lieutenant Commander
W. Rooke RAN (retd)

FAST FACT

Sailors wear a white uniform in summer and navy blue in winter. White uniforms evolved from the earliest days of naval uniforms when dyes were not available to add colour to the cotton used to make the clothing!

The Sailor Suit and the Blue Jean Square Rig Collar

The sailor suit, which sailors call the 'Blues' or 'Whites', is worn by junior sailors. It is used on special occasions and ceremonies and dates from the18th century. According to tradition, the blue jean square rig collar dates from when seamen wore their hair in tarred pigtails, although there is some debate over this. Sometimes it is hard to determine just how a tradition began! Some people think that touching the collar brings good luck. In 1846 Prince Albert was four years old when he first wore a sailor suit to match the sailors on the Royal Yacht. From then on, sailor suits became very popular clothing for children!

Chapter 11

ANIMALS & MASCOTS

Kuga is a military working dog who has been awarded a gallantry medal!

Animals and Mascots

Animals such as horses, dogs, camels, pigeons and elephants have been used in war for all sorts of purposes, from transport to communication. Animals have also been used as mascots in all three Services of the ADF. Some mascots play a role in ceremonies and may reflect a unit's role or location where it was formed or operated. A mascot does not have a job but instead provides companionship and boosts morale, becoming a symbol of the unit's identity. Some think they bring good luck.

Mascots can be official or unofficial. In World War I and World War II, many military units had unofficial mascots which were often stray animals, while others travelled from Australia with the soldiers such as kangaroos, wallabies and koalas. Dogs were common and some helped stretcher-bearers find wounded men.

Official and unofficial mascots are kept today and include dogs, horses, camels, a ram, a goanna, an eagle, a kookaburra, a cockatoo, a falcon and a rooster, along with a lion, tiger and crocodile! Sometimes mascots are kept in zoos and not on a military base!

Sergeant Septimus Quartus, the 1st Battalion Royal Australian Regiment's Mascot being led onto a parade ground.

Buzz and Wombat

In World War II, members of RAAF No 3 Squadron were operating in North Africa. They adopted a local monkey as a mascot and called it 'Buzz'. In the 1970s and 1980s, No 38 Squadron had the radio call sign 'Wombat'. They decided to appoint a wombat from Sydney's Taronga Park Zoo as their mascot.

Henri

In World War I, No 4 Squadron, AFC, was serving in France. On Christmas Day, a young boy called Henri Heremene wandered into the squadron's dinner. Henri's parents had been killed during the war. He was nicknamed 'Digger' and became the squadron's mascot. Private T.W. Tovell cared for him, smuggled him onto the ship that brought them back to Australia and later adopted Henri as his own child.

'Digger' Tovell on his motorcycle at the RAAF Base at Point Cook in 1928. He was unofficially apprenticed as a motor mechanic by RAAF.

Henri's story is one of great survival, but it is also quite tragic. Can you find out why?

The Ship's Cat called Red Lead

Ship's Cat, HMAS *Kanimbla* (AWM 300848)

Cats were kept on ships for hundreds of years to catch rats and mice. They were also thought to bring good luck and protection from bad weather. Red Lead was a kitten when it became HMAS *Perth*'s mascot in January 1942 during World War II. In late February, the ship came under attack from Japanese planes. Red Lead was terrified and hid in the captain's cabin. When HMAS *Perth* returned to harbour the sailors were dismayed to report that Red Lead tried to escape at least three times. It was thought to be bad luck for a cat to leave a ship. The next day HMAS *Perth* was engaged in battle by the Japanese navy and was sunk. Red Lead and over 350 men lost their lives.

Cats were banned from RAN ships in 1975 for hygiene reasons. Sailors brought stuffed toys instead to ensure the tradition continued.

Quintus

Corporal Rama (courtesy 5RAR)

The 5th Battalion of the Royal Australian Regiment (5 RAR) was formed in 1965 and allocated the unit colours of gold and black, the colours of a tiger. The battalion was nicknamed the 'Tiger Battalion'. A tiger cub from Sydney's Taronga Park Zoo was at the wharf to welcome 5 RAR when it returned to Australia from the Vietnam War in 1967. He was named Quintus (based on a Latin word meaning 'five') and became the regiment's mascot. Quintus was 'enrolled' in the army and the troops of 5 RAR gave financial support to the zoo for his upkeep. The battalion has continued the tradition of a tiger mascot ever since. The most recent was named Corporal Quintus Rama and lived at Crocodylus Park in Darwin. Corporal Rama passed away in 2019 at the age of 17 after serving 5 RAR for six years. His job description included attending ceremonial events and boosting morale.

Corporal John MacArthur 'Stan the Ram' of the 8th/9th Battalion RAR (courtesy Department of Defence)

Horrie the War Dog (AWM 076877)

FAST FACT!

In World War II an article in an Army magazine reported that servicemen had attempted to return to Australia with around 10 goats, 220 dogs, 170 cats, 150 birds and 50 monkeys and squirrels!

Horrie

Horrie was the unofficial mascot of the 1st Machine Gun Battalion during World War II. The dog was found by Private Jim Moody in the Egyptian desert. Horrie travelled to Greece, Crete, Palestine and Syria before arriving in Australia in 1942. The soldiers made Horrie his own uniform to keep him warm. He could identify the approach of enemy aircraft, survived the sinking of a boat and was wounded by a bomb fragment. Jim smuggled Horrie into Australia in a special pack. Three years later he was discovered by quarantine officials and was destroyed in 1945. There is a theory that Horrie was replaced by another dog from the pound and that Horrie lived the rest of his life at Corryong in Victoria.

Chapter 12

UNDERSTANDING OUR PAST

There are so many customs and traditions of the ADF that it is impossible to cover them all in a single book. There are both ceremonial and daily activities and behaviours that defence personnel perform that have histories dating back to ancient times. On Anzac Day and Remembrance Day we see just some of them. Knowing how these behaviours originated helps us to understand and appreciate the value they have in the lives of service personnel — for discipline, to develop a sense of belonging and positive values, for inspiration and pride in the service of the ADF.

Look around you in your daily life and you will see customs and traditions everywhere — at school, when visiting friends, or at sporting and cultural events. Think about why people or groups display certain behaviours. These may range from the clothing they wear, the food they eat on special days, a Welcome to Country, a religious ceremony, a festival, or your best friend's birthday!

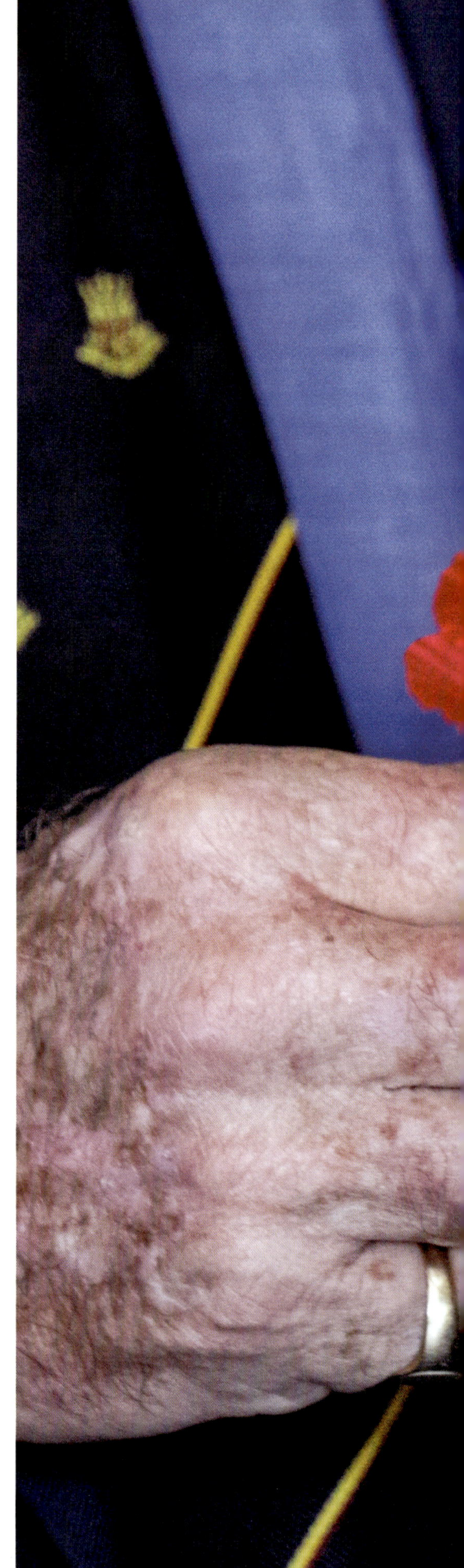

Customs and traditions are important to the people who perform them, and all have a history. Understanding that history can help us to appreciate and respect the people, organisations and groups who share our wonderful country of Australia.

A student reflects (courtesy of St Andrew's Anglican College).

A veteran remembers (courtesy of St Andrew's Anglican College).

Chapter 13

ACTIVITIES

Make A Family Flag

Flags are made up of different sections.

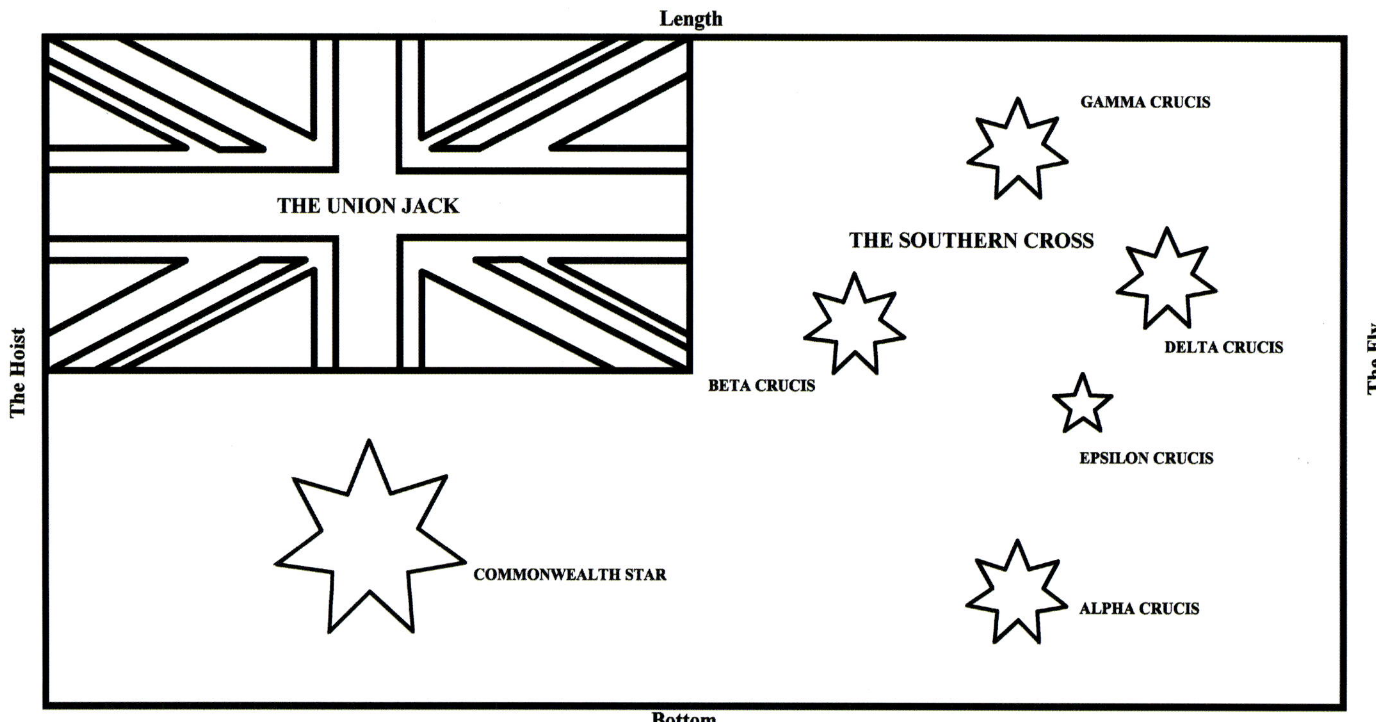

Using an A4 piece of paper, fold in four and design your own family flag.

What colours will you use?

What symbols will you use?

Make a Family or Class Medal of Courage

Look at the Cross of Valour medal. What is valour? How does the design of the medal represent valour?

Copy the template below.

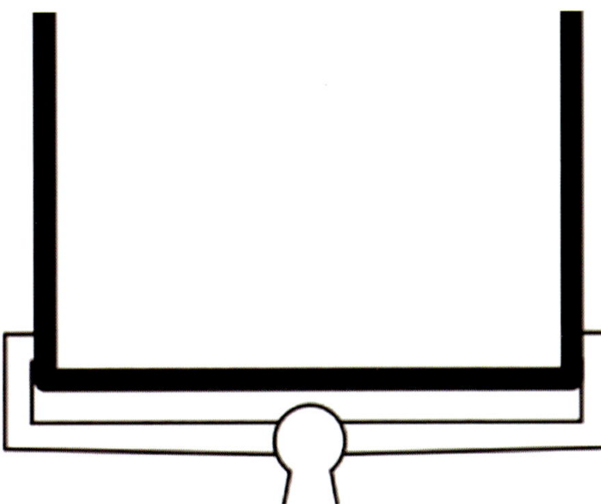

What three colours will you choose for the ribbon?

What symbols will you use?

Customs and Traditions of My Family
Mini Book

You will need:

- A4 Paper
- Stapler
- Pencils

Fold your paper in 4 and cut along the shortest fold line. Staple the two pieces of paper along the remaining fold line.

It could include the following chapter headings:

1. **This is my family.** Draw the members of your family.

2. **Customs & Traditions at Home.** The special events we celebrate or commemorate at home. Describe and draw about what you do.

3. **Community Customs & Traditions.** The special events we celebrate or commemorate in our community. Describe and draw what you do.

4. **Our Clothing.** The clothes we wear. Describe and draw.

5. **Our Food.** Food we like to make and eat. Describe and draw.

6. **Our Family Customs.** Other activities that are customs in your family such as holidays, games and family songs. Describe and draw.

Create a Coat of Arms

The Australia Service Medal 1939–1945 has the Australian Coat of Arms on the reverse. Research and find an image of the Commonwealth Coat of Arms. What symbols do you see? Why were they chosen?

Design a Coat of Arms for your family or class using the template below:

Chapter 14

Accoutrements – decorative pieces worn on uniforms.

Acronym – a word formed from the first letters of each word in a phrase.

ADF – Australian Defence Force.

ANZAC – An acronym representing the combined Australian and New Zealand Forces, first used in 1915 in Egypt and at Gallipoli. The earliest use of the word 'Anzac' was also in 1915.

Armistice – an agreement or truce between countries at war to stop the conflict and discuss conditions for peace.

Australian Imperial Force (AIF) – the volunteer Australian military force that served overseas in World War I. In World War II it was known as the 2nd AIF.

Campaign – military plans and combat actions aiming to resolve a conflict.

Cenotaph – means 'empty tomb' and is a monument built to represent those killed in war.

Conflict – disagreements between people or groups such as a struggle for power or property.

Culture – beliefs, customs and lifestyle of a group of people or a society.

Corps – a combined army unit or group that work together. It is pronounced as 'core'.

Country – a place of heritage, culture and belonging which, in Aboriginal culture, includes the land, sea, sky, rivers, seasons, plants and animals.

Customs – a way of behaving in certain circumstances, or doing something that is common to a group of people, a society, place, or time.

Dignitary – someone who holds a high-ranking position or rank.

Ensign – another name for a flag or banner.

Flotilla – a number of small naval vessels that are part of a larger fleet.

Memorial – something designed to honour an event, group of people or a person who has died.

Mourning – to grieve for someone who has died, or for the loss of something valued.

Peacekeeping – armed forces keeping the peace between groups or countries in conflict.

RAAF - Royal Australian Air Force.

RAN - Royal Australian Navy.

Regiment - a military unit of ground force soldiers.

Royal Decree – a command or decision made by the King or Queen.

Servicemen and women – men and women who serve in the armed forces.

Squadron – a part of, or unit of a naval fleet, armoured cavalry or air force.

Symbol – an action, object, event, picture etc that has special meaning and represents something else.

Traditions – customs, beliefs, legends, stories etc. that are handed down from one generation to another.

Union Jack – the flag of the United Kingdom representing its countries of England, Scotland, Wales and Northern Ireland. It is also called the Union Flag.

Unit – an individual group of soldiers that make up a larger group.

Chapter 15

INDEX

BIBLIOGRAPHY

90 Years of the RAAF: a snapshot History: Royal Australian Air Force (2011) Office of Air Force History, Commonwealth of Australia, Canberra

Admiralty Manual of Seamanship Vol. 1 (1964), Her Majesty's Stationery Office, London

Australian Army History Unit (2017) A Brief History of the Australian Army, Big Sky Publishing, Newport, NSW

Australian War Memorial (2011) *A Place to Remember*, Australia War Memorial, Canberra

Campbell, A.B. (1956) *Customs and Traditions of the Royal Navy*, Gale and Polden Limited, Aldershot, UK

Cassells, V. (2000) *The Capital Ships: Their Battles and their Badges*, Kangaroo Press, Roseville, NSW

Hampshire, A.C. (1979) *Just an Old Navy Custom*, William Kimber, London

James, Martin (ed.) *The Origins of the Royal Australian Air Force Customs & Traditions*, Office of Air Force History, File Ref: fB364158.

Jobson, C. (2009) *Looking Forward Looking Back: Customs and Traditions of the Australian Army*, Big Sky Publishing, Wavell Heights, QLD

Odgers, G (1989) *The RAAF: An Illustrated History*, Child and Associates Publishing, Frenchs Forest

Odgers, G (1993) *Navy Australia*, Department of Defence, Child and Associates Publishing, Frenchs Forest

McDonald, J (2018) *Shades of Blue*, RAAN History and Heritage Branch, Canberra

Paterson, A.M. (2014) *Anzac Sons: The Story of Five Brothers in the War to End All Wars, Big Sky Publishing*, Newport, NSW

Paterson, A.M. (2015) *Anzac Sons: Five Brothers on the Western Front*, Big Sky Publishing, Newport, NSW

Terrett, L.C. & Taubert S.C. (2011) *Preserving Our Proud Heritage: The Customs and Traditions of the Australian Army*, Big Sky Publishing, Newport, NSW

Websites:

Royal Australian Air Force: www.airforce.com.au

Australian Army: www.army.gov.au

Royal Australian Navy: www.navy.com.au

Australian Defence Force: www.defence.gov.au

Australian War Memorial: www.awm.gov.au

ACKNOWLEDGEMENTS

A child's thirst for knowledge knows few limits. As both a parent and teacher, I doubt there has been an Anzac Day or Remembrance Day service where I have not been asked a question that usually begins with the word 'why'. My response has often been 'I'm not really sure, but maybe we can find out.' In compiling *Australia Remembers: Customs and Traditions of the Australian Defence Force* I was motivated by those questions. There were also queries of my own that arose in the compilation of volume one of the **Australia Remembers** series, *Anzac Day, Remembrance Day and War Memorials.* The investigation to find the answers led me into a heritage so steeped with tradition that it was impossible to know where to draw the line. Ultimately, the questions of the children were my measure, so thank you to every curious child who wondered why.

My thanks to the team at the Australian Army History Unit, including Sophie Jerapetritis and Miesje de Vogel, for their support and fact checking of all things Army. To Les Terrett and Steve Taubert, the authors of *Preserving Our Proud Heritage: The Customs and Traditions of the Australian Army,* an incredibly detailed Australian Army History Unit compilation published by Big Sky Publishing and the first reference for the *Australia Remembers* series. In addition, I'd like to thank the research and publications team of the Australian War Memorial for bringing history to life and ensuring its accessibility.

My particular gratitude goes to the following individuals who gave their time to assist as we sifted through the volumes of information, stories and images: Commander

Max Hancock RAN (retd) who spent many hours refining the manuscript with a naval viewpoint, answering endless questions and providing leads; Group Captain David Fredericks, Director History and Heritage Services RAAF for all his support on RAAF history along with Warrant Officer Geoff Banning. Mr David Gardner, Director, RAAF Museum, RAAF Base Point Cook, who cheerfully led me through the collection and did not tire of my queries; Mr Martin James, Director of History – Air Force and RAAF Historian for providing access to his draft *The Origins of the Royal Australian Air Force Customs & Traditions* and Lieutenant Commander W. Rooke RAN (retd) for his reflections. Thanks also to the Royal Australian Navy and the Naval History Section of the Sea Power Centre – Australia, the Australian Army, the Royal Australian Air Force and the Australian Defence Force for permissions and guidance.

My sincere thanks to all those who provided assistance with sourcing photos: the Editor of the Navy News – Richard Mihaich; Sue Sagar and the staff of St Andrew's Anglican College (Peregian Springs), Amy Paterson, Rebecca Gray, Kerrin Yates and Jacinta Leo. Likewise, my thanks to my parents, Joan and Noel Marlow and my husband Rob, who not only take great photos, but offer enduring encouragement, support and honest comment, as do all the family! To my beta-readers, Rob Paterson, Daniel Gray and Lyn Rees, my sincere gratitude. Thanks also to those service personnel and children who responded to our call for reflections on the value of customs and traditions.

I would like to offer my endless appreciation to Denny Neave, Sharon Evans and Diane Evans at Big Sky Publishing, along with their talented design team, Pat and Chris. Your dedication to the preservation of Australia's history is inspirational. Much gratitude also to Cathy McCullagh, a very forgiving and patient editor whose experience, skill and insight are greatly respected and valued, as is her friendship.

To my extended family of today and those who came before, particularly Sarah, Charles, Jim, Charlie, George, Allan, Percy and Albert Marlow, thank you.

ABOUT THE AUTHOR

Allison Paterson is the author of the 2016 ABIA and CBCA-longlisted title *Anzac Sons: Five Brothers on the Western Front*, the children's version of the adult non-fiction title *Anzac Sons: the Story of Five Brothers in the War to End All Wars*. Both are based on a collection of over 500 letters sent from the Western Front by her grandfather and his four brothers. Her children's picture books, *Granny's Place* and *Shearing Time*, are inspired by childhood memories of her grandparents and life on the farm. *Australia Remembers: Anzac Day, Remembrance Day and War Memorials* is the first volume in the Australia Remembers series and was published in 2018. Allison was a teacher-librarian for over 20 years and has reviewed children's literature for *Magpies Magazine* for almost as long. She was a recipient of a 2017 May Gibbs Children's Literature Trust Creative Time Fellowship. The resulting young adult manuscript *Follow After Me* was released in 2019. Allison now works as a writer, presenter and publishing consultant.

To invite Allison to visit your school she can found at:
www.allisonmarlowpaterson.com

Available now online or at all good bookstores

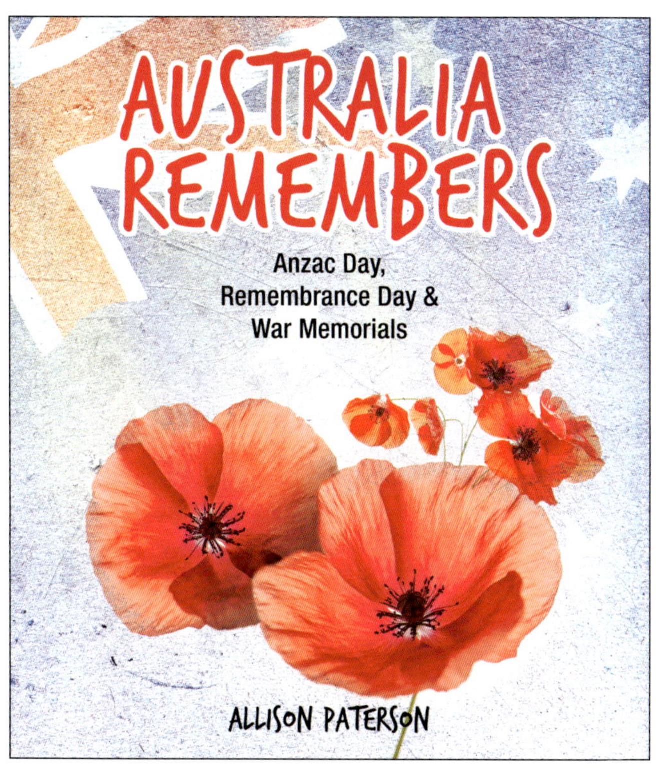

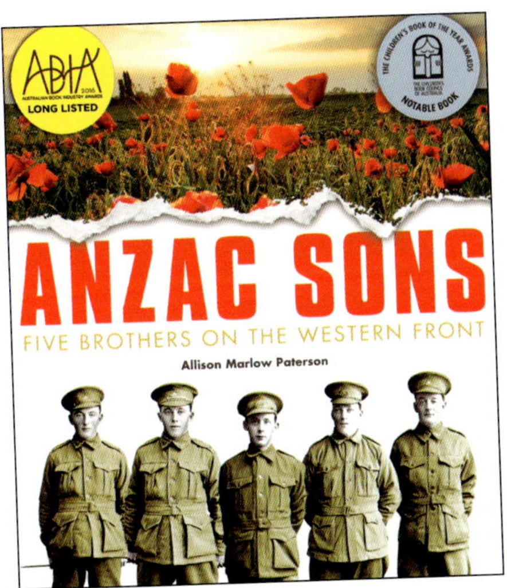

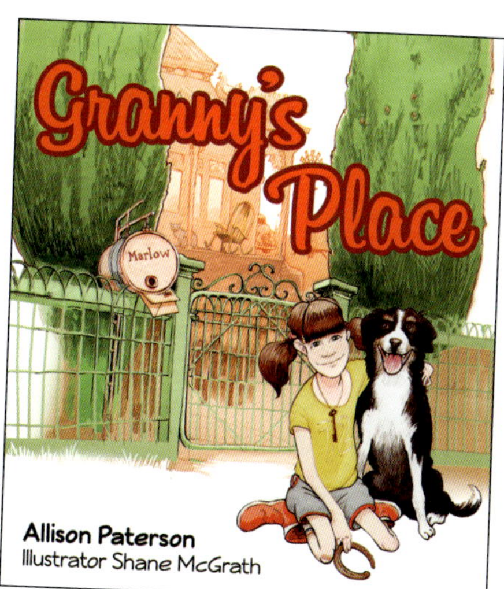

View sample pages, reviews and information on this book and other titles at **www.bigskypublishing.com.au**

More Great Books from Big Sky Publishing

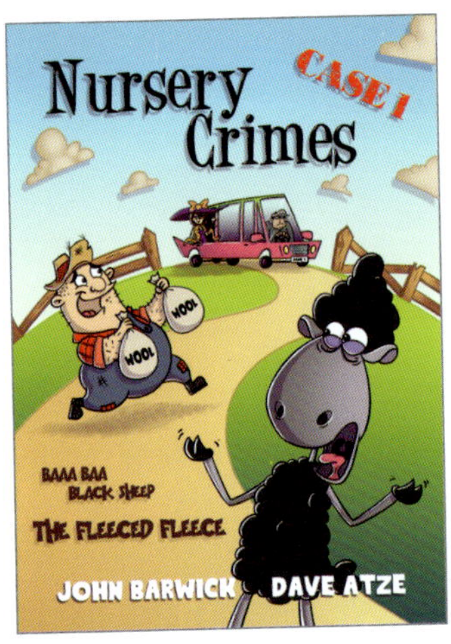

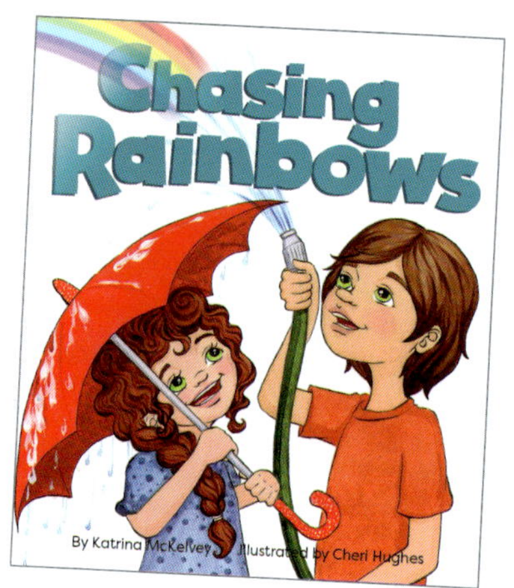

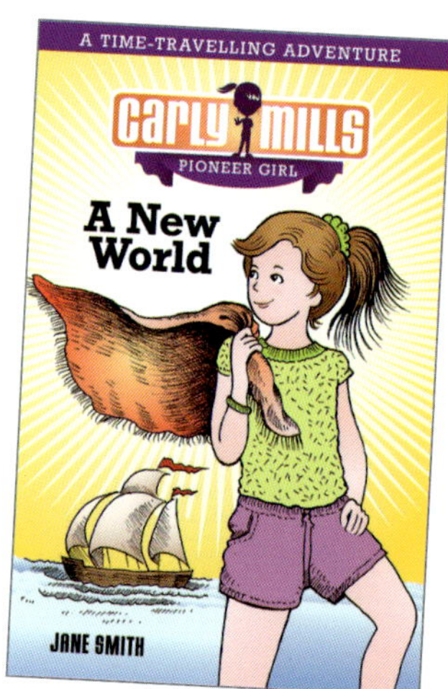

View sample pages, reviews, teachers' notes and information on this book and other titles at **www.bigskypublishing.com.au**

BIG SKY PUBLISHING